THE SPORTSTOWN SERIES
EDITED BY RICHARD A. JOHNSON

The Boston Braves, 1871–1953
Harold Kaese

Dynasty's End: Bill Russell and the 1968–69
World Champion Boston Celtics
Thomas J. Whalen

Ted Williams: Reflections on a Splendid Life
Lawrence Baldassaro

Francis Ouimet with his ten-year-old caddie, Eddie Lowery,
U.S. Open, 1913. Courtesy of the Ouimet Foundation

A Game of Golf

Francis Ouimet

FOREWORD BY BEN CRENSHAW

INTRODUCTION AND PHOTO SELECTION
BY RICHARD A. JOHNSON

AFTERWORD BY ROBERT DONOVAN

Northeastern University Press
BOSTON

First published in 1932 by Houghton Mifflin

LIBRARY OF CONGRESS CATALOGING-IN-PUBLICATION-DATA
Ouimet, Francis.
A game of golf / Francis Ouimet ; foreword by Ben Crenshaw;
introduction and photo selection by Richard A. Johnson ;
afterword by Robert Donovan.   Northeastern University Press ed.
p. cm. (The sportsman series)
ISBN 1–55553–600–x (pbk. : alk. paper)
1. Ouimet, Francis. 2. Golfers United States Biography.
3. Golf—Anecdotes. I. Title. II. Series.
GV964.O8 2004
796.352′092 — dc22   2004005640

Printed and bound by Edwards Brothers, Inc.,
in Ann Arbor, Michigan.

This paper is EB Natural, an acid-free sheet.

Manufactured in the United States of America

08 07 06 05 04 5 4 3 2 1

CONTENTS

ILLUSTRATIONS

SPORTSTOWN SERIES PREFACE

IT'S BEEN SAID that you can judge a city by its newspapers, bars, ballparks, and bookstores. By this reasonable standard Boston is world-class. Boston is to sports and literature what Paris is to painting and romance, London to drama and royalty, and Rome to ruins and traffic.

Sporting traditions dictate both the landscape and the social calendar of Bostonians. They literally plan their lives around The Marathon, The Beanpot, The Country Club, The Green Monster, and The Game. Not only has Boston produced and embraced the talents of such athletes as John L. Sullivan, Bobby Orr, Sam Langford, Joan Benoit, Bill Russell, and Ted Williams, but it is also the city which boasts of writers such as Phillis Wheatley, Nathaniel Hawthorne, William Dean Howells, Henry James, John Updike, and Edwin O'Connor, to name but a few. It is no surprise that sportswriting developed in Boston and that the writers documenting the local sports scene have nearly matched the accomplishments of both their writing and athletic counterparts. For generations the sports pages of Boston's many newspapers have been among the best in America. Likewise, books depicting Boston's colorful and unparalleled array of athletes, events, and teams are among the best of world sports literature.

For years many of these books have been out of print. The Sportstown Series from Northeastern University Press, selected and edited by myself, an author and the curator of The Sports Museum in Boston, reprints selected works among these classics and publishes original titles that illuminate one of the world's great sports regions. Following our well-received first volume, *Ted Williams: Reflections on a Splendid Life*, edited by Lawrence Baldassaro, came *Dynasty's End: Bill Russell and the 1968–69 World Champion Boston Celtics*, by Tom Whalen, and *The Boston Braves, 1871–1953*, by Harold Kaese. Now we offer Francis Ouimet's memoir, *A Game of Golf*, as the fourth installation in our developing Sportstown Series.

RICHARD A. JOHNSON

FOREWORD

MY COPY of Francis Ouimet's *A Game of Golf* was given to me at The Country Club in 1968 at the USGA Junior Championship. It remains one of my dearest possessions. The jacket is a little tattered and worn, but its contents are just as exciting as the first time I thumbed through the pages. It reveals a completely different era of golf, with great triumphs, heartbreaking losses, and the passion for playing the game at the top level. The matches come alive so clearly, that a reader becomes a spectator.

Francis Ouimet, helped by his kind brother Wilfred, started the game on a little course in the back of their home near the seventeenth hole at The Country Club. It's ironic that young Francis, with his modest upbringing, would make history so nearby, in an entirely different world. During that incredible week in September 1913 a legend materialized. Ouimet, who was a local success but relatively untried in national competitions, beat the two best British players at the time, Harry Vardon and Ted Ray, in a playoff for the U.S. Open title.

American golf was never the same after that week, but Ouimet would always remain modest, humble, and unassuming. Throughout his life, he retained a great capacity for making and keeping friends wherever he went. Ouimet triumphed with imperturbable play, but the story contains a greater dimension of innocence with the ten-year-old caddie Eddie Lowery. Constantly, the boy reminded Francis, "Keep your eye on the ball." What golfer could not benefit from this advice? The image of the two lads striding down a fairway provides a lasting one for us and enabled them to keep a lifelong friendship with each other and the game of golf.

The year following his U.S. Open title, Ouimet won the U.S. Amateur at Ekwanok in Vermont. Seventeen years later, after eight Walker Cups and a handful of defeats in the semifinals of the Amateur, he won perhaps the most satisfying victory of his career at Beverly Hills, Illinois. He thereafter devoted himself to business and raising his two daughters in Boston.

Ouimet founded the Francis Ouimet Scholarship Fund in 1949. The scholarship that bears his name provides incalculable goodwill through golf and allows young people a chance to succeed through sound education. This will always be Francis Ouimet's most important achievement, even greater than having been the first American to be named captain of the Royal and Ancient Golf Club in St. Andrews in 1951.

For me, being named captain in 1999 for the Ryder Cup was a great honor. The Country Club provided a basis for learning golf history, golf course

architecture, and an introduction to serious golf.
After our team staged a furious rally to win the cup,
I brought two things back with me: a miniature
bronze of Francis Ouimet and Eddie Lowery from
the Ryder Cup caddies, and the eerie feeling that
Francis Ouimet's spirit guided Justin Leonard's putt
into the seventeenth hole that electric afternoon.
No one can convince me otherwise.

BEN CRENSHAW
AUSTIN, TEXAS
JANUARY 2004

PREFACE

GOLFER FRANCIS OUIMET'S groundbreaking triumph in the 1913 U.S. Open was a true measure of the lasting significance of a historical event. The images depicting that day framed his impact on the game of golf and also revealed his character.

The most famous of these images is of Ouimet at age twenty, following a drive on the day in which he forced a playoff against British legends Harry Vardon and Ted Ray. With his driver in hand, he strides beside his caddie, ten-year-old, four-foot-tall Eddie Lowery. His expression is one of purpose as the two approach their second shot. Ouimet with his unaffected gaze and Lowery, his stoic figure toting a bag nearly his size, continue to inspire both golfers and non-golfers alike.

Minutes after this photograph was shot, Ouimet rejected a fellow competitor's offers to caddie the playoff round in favor of Lowery, who, standing at the periphery of the multitude congratulating Ouimet, was tearful upon hearing the entreaties. Ultimately, Ouimet's character and easy personality became the most visible and important component of his legacy.

After more than a century of American golf, Ouimet emerges as the winner of the big event, the great victory that introduced the game to these shores. He was the first non-Briton selected as the captain of the Royal and Ancient Golf Club at St. Andrews, and he is the author of one of the greatest books ever published on the game.

It is with pride that the Sportstown Series presents this edition of Francis Ouimet's memoirs, *A Game of Golf*. His gentle nature, native wisdom, and love for the game glow on each page, and his prose is as direct and honest as the boy who grew up in the shadow of the seventeenth hole of The Country Club, and the champion who achieved his greatness at that same hole.

As his British colleagues undoubtedly said, "It was all great stuff," and remains so to this day.

Enjoy.

RICHARD A. JOHNSON
EDITOR, THE SPORTSTOWN SERIES

A GAME OF GOLF

.:.

CHAPTER I

ACROSS THE STREET FROM
THE COUNTRY CLUB

BORN in a rather thinly populated section of Brookline, Massachusetts, I have often wondered what my golfing activities would have amounted to if my father had not bought a home bordering on the Country Club. Of one thing I am quite certain, and that is I should never have had the opportunity of developing an interest in the game of golf to the same extent that was made possible by close proximity to a fine course. As it was, daily trips from home to a little schoolhouse, built in 1768 and known as the Putterham School, carried me back and forth across the fairways. Not that I was granted any such privileges, but in the rôle of a trespasser I discovered that this route saved many footsteps, got me to school on time, and, more important, enabled me to get home with the least possible delay.

There was a more intriguing motive, however. Frequently on one of my excursions I ran across a lost ball, of the gutta-percha variety. At the age of seven I had a collection of Silvertowns, Ocobos, Vardon Flyers, Henleys, and other brands popular among golfers in 1900 that would do full credit to the professional's shop.

Long before I ever had a club, I had golf balls enough to last me for years. But the balls without a club were not very useful. Golf was so new to America in 1900 that it was difficult to get clubs. They never got lost, and were rarely discarded. The balls, however, seemed to have plenty of life in them, their varied markings held some sort of fascination for me, and it was fun watching them bound from rocks and other solid substances.

After I had hoarded golf balls enthusiastically for two years, someone gave my brother Wilfred a club. When Wilfred was busy caddying, I helped myself to that club and used it to knock some of my hoard around the back yard. I was careful to put Wilfred's club back in its place before he put in an appearance. Otherwise, I felt, there might have been a family riot. Occasionally a tournament was held at the Country Club and on those days and after school, I would stand on the edge of a fairway and watch the golfers go by. If I saw someone play an exceptional stroke, I watched how he did it and hastened home to take Wilfred's club and set about trying to put into practice what I had seen. Those efforts must have been funny, but they were, after all, the beginnings of my game, such as it is.

I can remember vividly the first Haskell ball I ever found. It was in the fall of 1902, and I was nine years old. Wilfred was a caddie boy at the Country Club, and the ladies were having their national championship. On the way home from school, I picked up a nice new ball. It was unlike any other I had ever seen and seemed much livelier. I showed it to Wilfred and he told me it was one of the new rubber-cored balls. Few had them, and Big Brother tried his best to talk me into parting with it. Nothing doing. I played with it, bounced it, and used it until the paint wore off. I got some white paint and painted it. Mother was baking some bread in a hot oven and I sneaked my repainted Haskell into the oven, thinking the heat would dry the ball.

Mother smelled something burning and went all through the house trying to discover the cause. She found nothing, but the odor was so strong, and she was so worried that the house was burning up, that she kept on searching. Finally she opened the oven door and the most awful smell in the world came out of the newly made batch of bread. It was ruined — and so was my prize, the Haskell. The heat had melted the gutta-percha shell and there was nothing left of the thing but a shriveled-up mass of elastic bands. I learned then and there

3

how Doctor Haskell made his golf balls and why it was that the rubber-cored ball was vastly superior to the solid gutta.

The Haskell crowded the gutta off the courses and made the game much more enjoyable to play. At any rate, I could play the rubber-cored better than the hard ones, and my interest in the game increased. Behind our house was a cow pasture, and here Wilfred, with the mind of a golf architect, built three holes. The first was about a hundred and fifty yards long, with a carry over a brook. The brook was a hundred yards or so from where we drove. When he hit a shot well, Wilfred could drive close to the green, but it was far beyond my reach. As a matter of fact, the very best I could do was to drive into the brook. The second hole was very short, hardly more than fifty yards. The last was a combination of the first two, and brought the player back to the starting-point. We used tomato cans for hole rims. As I visualize that old course of ours, it was the most difficult one I have ever played because it contained a gravel pit, swamps, brooks, and patches of long grass. We — or rather Wilfred — had selected only the high and dry pieces of land, which were few and far between, to play over. A shot that traveled three yards off line meant a lost ball, and it was well we had plenty!

Wilfred made trips to Boston from time to time

and discovered that Wright and Ditson had a golf department with a man named Alex Findlay in charge. He discovered also that a good club could be got in exchange for used golf balls, and that three dozen would be a fair exchange for the best club made. From one of these visits Wilfred brought me home a mashie, and for the first time in my young life I was independent so far as playing golf was concerned. I had my own club, balls, and a place to play. What more could anyone ask!

A lawnmower kept two of the greens in fair condition, but the one near our house was used so much it was worn bare and had no grass whatsoever on it. You see, while we were waiting for a meal we fiddled around the hole and the grass never had a chance to grow. One advantage, from Mother's point of view, was that she always knew where to look, and it was a simple matter for her to call us into the house. We fooled around that particular spot early in the morning and long after dark, and it was small wonder that my interest in golf increased because, with all this practice, it was natural enough that I should notice some improvement in my play. Mother thought I had gone crazy because golf was the only thing I seemed interested in.

I had more time to devote to the game than Wilfred. He had chores to do around the house

5

and barn and being older, he was the one called upon to go on errands. They say practice makes perfect, and I believe it. After striving for weeks and months to hit a ball over the brook, and losing many, I finally succeeded. A solid year of practice had enabled me to drive accurately, if not far, and one Saturday morning, after trying for an hour, I drove a ball as clean as a whistle beyond the brook.

When I told Wilfred of my accomplishment, he received my story with a good deal of doubt. I had now acquired a brassie to go with the mashie, and I invited my brother out to the pasture to see what I could do with it. Whether I was tired out from my earlier efforts or not, I do not know, but I failed utterly, and Wilfred naturally was more skeptical than ever. The next day was Sunday, and after I returned from Sunday School, I went at it again. This time Wilfred was with me, and I definitely convinced him by hitting two balls out of three over the brook. It soon got to be a habit, and I was quite disgusted with myself when I failed.

A good many tournaments were held at the Country Club and the best golfers gathered to play in them. Soon I was old enough to caddie, and as a youngster of eleven I saw in action such great golfers as Arthur Lockwood, Chandler Egan, Fred Herreshoff, Jerry Travers, and Walter J. Travis among the amateurs, and Alex Campbell, the

Country Club professional, Alex Smith, Tom McNamara, Willie Anderson, and many of the prominent professional players. If I noticed anything particularly successful in the play of any of these golfers, I made a mental note of it, and when opportunity afforded, I set out to my private course and practiced the things I had noted.

Therefore, you see, I was brought up in a golfing environment and learned to love the game. I read in magazines or newspapers anything I could find relating to golf, got a few of the boys in the neighborhood interested in the game, and jumped into it head over heels. One day I caddied for a dear old gentleman named Samuel Carr. Mr. Carr was a golfing enthusiast, and, furthermore, always most considerate of the boy who carried his clubs. All the boys liked him. Playing the eighteenth or last hole one day, he asked me if I played golf. I told him I did.

He asked me if I had any clubs. I replied that I had two, a brassie and mashie.

'When we finish, I wish you would come to the locker room with me; I may have a few clubs for you,' he said.

I took Mr. Carr's clubs downstairs to the caddie shop and hustled back. He came out with four clubs under his arm, a driver with a leather face, a lofter, a midiron, and a putter. I think it was the biggest thrill I had ever got up to that time.

7

Early mornings — and when I say early I mean around four-thirty or five o'clock — I abandoned my own course and played a few holes on that of the Country Club, until a greenskeeper drove me away. Rainy days, when I was sure no one would be around, I would do the same thing. Complaints concerning my activities arrived home, and Mother warned me to keep off the course, usually ending her reprimand by saying that the game of golf was bound to get me into trouble.

I was so wrapped up in the game, however, I just couldn't let it alone. One summer, tired of my own layout, I talked a companion, Frank Mahan, into going to Franklin Park with me. Franklin Park was a public course and we could go there and play unmolested. We set out one Saturday morning. To get to Franklin Park, we had to walk a mile and a half with our clubs to the car line. Then we rode to Brookline Village, transferred there to a Roxbury Crossing car, arrived at Roxbury Crossing and changed again to a Franklin Park car. After getting out of the last street car, we walked about three quarters of a mile to the clubhouse, checked our coats — that is all we had to check — and then played six full rounds of the nine holes, a total of fifty-four holes.

Then we went home the way we had come, completely exhausted. All this at the age of thirteen!

Another thing I like to remember is the day I was

8

selected by Dan McNamara, the caddie master at
the Country Club, to act as caddie for a gentleman
named Theodore Hastings. Mr. Hastings was
peculiar about his golf: he invariably played alone.
As we walked toward the first tee, he asked me if
I played. I told him I did. He asked me where
I lived. I told him. He said, 'Get your clubs and
we will play a round.'

Of course, caddies were not permitted to play on
the course at all, but when Mr. Hastings invited
me, I forgot all about regulations, dashed home for
my set, and all running records were broken in
getting back to that first tee.

The Country Club course was not as difficult
then as now, but for all that it was one of the
leading courses in the country and was hard
enough for anyone. I played the first nine holes
in thirty-nine strokes, and Mr. Hastings was
considerably impressed. I not only lugged my
own clubs, but his as well and was having a marvelous time. The fifteenth hole passed directly by
the caddie house, and Dan McNamara usually
sat in a chair overlooking the caddie shed and
with a perfect view of the fifteenth fairway.
Furthermore, he was a disciplinarian. I have
since learned that a good caddie master has to be
one.

My play continued satisfactorily through the
fourteenth, but then I began to think of Dan! I hit

a good tee shot over the hill and, walking around, I cast a glance toward the caddie shed. There was Dan. I doubt if I have ever been as nervous before or since. I topped my second shot and missed the third. It was a simple hole to make in five. I put my fourth into a trap and needed three to get out. The hole cost me a ten.

Once out of Dan's sight, I steadied a bit and finished the round with a score of 84. Delighted beyond words, I was ready to meet Dan in all his fury. Mr. Hastings came to my assistance, though, signed my caddie check, and told Dan he had had a most enjoyable afternoon. Dan was reasonable, too, seemed interested to know what score I made and wanted to know also what happened to me on the fifteenth. I truthfully told him I expected to see him come running after me, and was just frightened to death.

Those are just a few of the highlights that brought me closer than ever to the game. As a grammar-school boy I was looking forward to the time when I should graduate and become enrolled in Brookline High School. In 1902, an association had been formed, known as the Greater Boston Golf Association, and all boys registered at a high or preparatory school were eligible to compete in the annual championship. My ambition was to play in this event and win it. Many a fine golfer was developed in this tournament. Percy Gilbert was a winner one year. So was Henry Wilder. George Bowden, a fine professional golfer, got his start in the schoolboy championship. Mike Brady played in it. Carl Anderson, Heinrich Schmidt, Ray Gorton — I can think of other good ones.

I was graduated from the Heath Grammar School in 1908, and of course the following September I should be in Brookline High School. Could I wait to become a full-fledged member of the high school? I should say not. The championship was to be played at Wollaston. In went my entry to the secretary, honestly feeling I could represent Brookline High because that was to be my school in two months. When I arrived at Wollaston, there was some question about my eligibility. I explained to Wilfred Shrigley, the secretary, that I intended to go to Brookline High in the fall. After a brief conference, my entry was accepted. I qualified in the championship division with a score of 85. Bill Flynn, now well known as a golf architect, led the field with a grand round of 74.

My first match was with a boy named J. H. Sullivan, Jr., and I managed to beat him. As a proof that he harbored no ill-feelings toward me, he later introduced me to his sister, and the young lady is now my wife. In the next round I was eliminated by Carl Anderson, a big burly fellow from Winthrop High School. Carl was a great chap. To make me feel at ease, he said, 'You can call me

11

Andy.' He could not pronounce my name and he let it go at just plain Francis.

We had a great match, but Andy was too good and beat me on the seventeenth green two up and one to play. I had the satisfaction of drawing out his best golf and found consolation in the thought that it took the champion to put me out. It was my first competition, and I had a wonderful time.

I spent the summer practicing and improved my play considerably — or at least I felt I had done so. Summer rolled along and it was soon time really to go to Brookline High School. Off and on I had played a little baseball, and other than to kick a football around I had little interest in that sport. The game never appealed to me because I weighed about a hundred and ten, and there were so many boys in school that were bigger and stronger, I decided to keep up my golfing interest.

There were several boys in school who liked to play golf, so we held a meeting and organized a golf team. Newton High School had a team. Roxbury Latin and Fessenden School also had teams. That golf team furnished many a laugh for the boys and girls in school. Two of the boys belonged to Woodland and a competition was arranged at this club to determine the team of five to represent the School on the golf course. The competition consisted of an eighteen-hole medal contest, the five low scorers being rewarded. I happened to be the leader and was placed number one. The manager, Harry McDougal, arranged the schedule, and we had matches twice a week with neighboring schools on different courses.

One of the first matches played was with the Fessenden School. This was a private school on the Albemarle golf course in Newtonville. John G. Anderson, who had won the Massachusetts State amateur championship in 1907 and has since been a national and international figure in golf, was teaching English at Fessenden and incidentally interesting the boys in golf. All they had to do was to step out of the school and they were on the course. John also arranged the matches.

We had no automobiles and had to get around after school to the various golf courses in street cars. When a match was to be played, we trudged off to school with our clubs and books and that was the signal to poke plenty of fun at the members of our golf team. The schedule of games was posted in the school paper, and in any study room where a member of the golf team sat could be seen such notices as these on the blackboard: 'The members of the marble team will play at Albemarle this afternoon.' Or, 'Candidates for the tiddledy-winks team will report at Woodland this P.M.' Our little golf team stood for plenty of ridicule, but we laughed it off, and cautiously sneaked our clubs in

13

the back way and checked them with the school janitor for use later in the day.

The day we were to play Fessenden School, we arrived at Albemarle about two-forty-five. John G. Anderson, English teacher, manager and captain of the Fessenden School team, was waiting for us. I submitted my list of players to John and he showed me his lineup. To my surprise his name was on the paper, and I politely informed him we came out to Albemarle to meet a school team and not the faculty.

'Well,' said John, with a smile on his face, 'there are only four boys in the school old enough to play on our team, and I make the fifth.' Since we had our team of five on hand, I was the lamb led to the slaughter. I was frightened to death because John Anderson was the first well-known golfer I ever competed against outside of scholastic circles. There were two lads on that Fessenden team who later developed into fine golfers. One was Philip Carter, who a few years ago made some unbelievable scores at Pinehurst, and the other a chubby youngster from far-off Honolulu named Francis Brown. I do not know what has happened to Phil Carter, but Brown is still rated very highly and performs brilliantly in the Hawaiian Islands and California, where he does most of his playing.

But to get back to our match. I had the honor and drove well down the fairway in spite of my excitement and nervousness. John topped his drive. That gave me a bit of courage, and I won the first hole. Albemarle in 1908 was short, and John's length availed him nothing because I reached greens about as quickly as he could and that day approached and putted like a demon. I finished with a 72, the best score I had ever made, and beat John five up and three to play. It was a wonderful experience, one I shall never forget, and John got fully as much pleasure out of it as myself.

It came on winter and our activities shifted to other sports. I was always interested in skating and ice hockey and went out for the school hockey team, but made little progress. My only thought was on golf, and that winter we made plans for our spring golf engagements. A schedule of matches was arranged and our team strengthened by the addition of Foggy Ainsworth, who later made a name for himself as a halfback on the Yale football team. Ellery Rogers was another who did well after he got out of school, on the golf team at Harvard.

We had many an interesting match with Newton High School, Roxbury Latin, Fessenden, and Worcester Classical High, and the spring rolled along rather quickly. Though each and every match was hard-fought and eagerly contested, there was nothing but the friendliest feeling toward one another and nothing of an unpleasant nature ever

15

cropped out. The schoolboy championship came along in July and was held at the Commonwealth Country Club. A fine field turned up, the boys coming from all parts of the State.

In connection with the qualifying round, a team championship was played, and the lowest aggregate of five scores from any school was declared the winner. There were not more than five or six schools who could gather enough entries for this contest, but Brookline High School succeeded in winning. I managed to qualify for the individual championship, although my score was somewhat blemished with a few bad holes, a nine in particular almost putting me out of the title play at the start.

To me the Greater Boston interscholastic championship was the most important golfing event in the world. After celebrating my sixteenth birthday in May, I stopped caddying, so that nothing should interfere with my competing as an amateur. In those days any boy who caddied after his sixteenth birthday was ineligible to play in the schoolboy event or any amateur tournament, but this rule has been changed recently and the age limit is now eighteen.

I worked my way to the final round after one or two close matches, and then went out to see who my opponent was to be. A group of caddie boys formed the gallery of the last semi-final match which was played between John Brady, representing Brighton High School, and Ronald Waitt, from Melrose High. It was a hard battle all the way, and Waitt finally holed a mean four-footer on the seventeenth green, to win. Incidentally John Brady was the younger brother of the famous Mike, who was professional at Commonwealth.

The final match was thirty-six holes. Ronald could hit a ball much farther than I, but he did not always hit it as accurately. I did not have the strength to swing hard, but what I lacked in distance I more than made up on and around the greens. Furthermore, Commonwealth was a comparatively short course and distance was not a prime essential. I won the championship by ten up and nine to play, and a happier boy never lived. I figured that was the ultimate in golf and there were no more worlds to conquer. I soon changed my mind.

Shortly after, the United States open championship was played at Englewood, New Jersey, and Tom McNamara finished second to George Sargent. I read every word that was written about the play, and, since Tom was a Bostonian and the brother of my old caddie master, Dan, I began to pay attention to national golf, but only as an interested enthusiast. Tom was the original homebred professional, the only American boy who had learned his golf in this country up to that time and capable of holding his own in fast company. With the open

17

championship at his mercy, he suffered a sunstroke and faded on the last three or four holes. So much was written in Boston newspapers concerning his play, it gave the game a great boost hereabouts and did more than anything else to interest me in national competition. As far as I was concerned, I wanted to play golf as an amateur, and, while amateurs competed in the open tournament, it was regarded as an event well beyond amateur ability and skill.

There was, however, a national amateur championship, and after my success in the interscholastic event, I secretly harbored an ambition to win that championship. More about it later.

On top of my interest in the game itself, I took a tremendous interest in the clubs and balls, particularly the latter. I had seen many changes in the golf ball, and I believe the great development in the game of golf is directly attributable to the wonderful strides made by the manufacturers in perfecting the ball and making the game a more pleasant one to play. As I have already said, the old hard and solid gutta-percha ball was succeeded by the rubber-filled Haskell. Then came the Kempshall Flyer. These balls were extremely resilient, but their qualities of durability were far from satisfactory.

I have seen both of these crack wide open and become unfit for play on the first or second shot.

If the golfer topped one of them, it was the finish. They just would not last at all. Then came a ball called the Spalding Wizard. But like the first two, it could not stand up under punishment. British-made balls put in an appearance and they were easily destroyed.

Along about 1906, the Goodyear people, who had helped Doctor Haskell in perfecting the original rubber-cored ball, placed on the market a ball called the Pneumatic. This ball had a rubber cover or shell into which air was compressed. It caught the fancy of the golfers for a time, but the Pneumatic had to be hit powerfully in order to get it along, and players in 1906 were new at the game and did not have the necessary hitting powers. The younger element had fair success with it, because they could hit harder and therefore got the better results. It lacked the resiliency of the rubber-cored balls, and although it was fairly durable in so far as cutting the cover was concerned, it had other faults which were distressing. Many times it was knocked out of shape, and when this did not occur, it exploded either in flight or in the caddie bags. Golfers had many interesting experiences with the Pneumatic.

With a view to improving the ball and making it indestructible, the Goodyear firm introduced in 1907 a ball called the Silk Pneumatic. It was constructed in this fashion: The cover was made of rubber, and inside were woven silken strands something along the idea of the automobile tire fabric. This strengthened the cover materially. Inside this was placed a substance resembling gelatine, in solid form and about a quarter of an inch thick. The gelatine layer fitted into the inner cover or shell. Then the air was pressed inside, and you had your ball. It was a big improvement over the Pneumatic, seemed a trifle more lively, and stood up reasonably well. Alex Campbell played the ball, as did Alex Smith and other well-known professionals of that time.

In 1907, Campbell was playing in the open championship at the Philadelphia Cricket Club and had a fine chance to win. He played two shots with his Silk Pneumatic to the edge of a green and took four more to hole out from about twenty feet. Picking his ball out of the cup, he discovered it had burst, the air had escaped, and he had been playing those four shots with nothing more nor less than a mushy bag. Those Pneumatic balls played better after they had been hammered around quite a bit, but there was always the danger that something would happen, and they were thrown into the discard.

In 1908 liquid-filled balls were made. Spalding put out a ball called the Aqua. Another was named Water Core. Before these innovations, the center of a golf ball consisted of a small piece of gutta-percha the size of a marble, and around this were wound the rubber or elastic bands. Balls with liquid centers were very popular, but manufacturers had much trouble making them durable. Nevertheless, they were far superior to the gutta.

Nowadays golf balls are made in two styles — either recessed or mesh-marked. With an exception here or there, all rubber-cored balls up to 1908 or 1909 had the bramble or pimple marking. I think it was in 1908 that this marking was inverted and became known as the Dimple. The Glory Dimple, with its red, white, and blue decoration, was a grand ball. And one more thing about golf balls: There has been so much comment in recent years about the size and weight of the golf ball. Those early rubber-cored balls were very light, floated in water, and no one gave a single thought to size or weight!

The clubs themselves came in for improvements. When I think of the beautiful clubs that are made now and compare them with some of the weapons that we handled twenty-odd years ago, I wonder how we ever did it. I suppose every club up to 1909 or 1910 was made by hand. I can vividly recall as a small boy peeking longingly through the window outside of Alex Campbell's shop at the Country Club, watching Alex, or his brothers, Matt and Andy, and Davey Brown fashion club heads out of plain blocks of wood, and scrape shafts by the hour until they were the proper size to insert in one of these wooden heads or irons. Everything was done by hand.

Just think of the time and work that went into the making of a driver! The block was shaped. Horn was fitted into the bottom of the driver. Hot lead was poured into the back to add weight. If a brassie was to be made, the same things were done, and a rough piece of brass hammered and pounded into a thin sheet and then fitted to the bottom and screwed on. Then the shaft was glued to the head, and after that, planed and tested to get the whip properly placed, then sand-papered, first with heavy sand-paper, then medium, and finally light. The leather grips were put on. The heads and shafts were stained. I can tell you it was arduous work, and it required skill and patience to build up a stock of clubs for sale.

Club-making in the golf shop today seems to be a lost art. Today shafts come through from the manufacturers the proper sizes. Heads — and I am thinking of wooden heads now — are practically finished. If you break a shaft or your club becomes unfit for play, it is no time before a new one can be replaced. Two or three years ago, playing the fifth hole, I happened to break a shaft in a favorite iron. I sent it back to the shop, and by the time I reached the ninth green, my club was there waiting for me. In the old days I should have had to wait a week for the same job because of orders ahead.

CHAPTER II

MY BEGINNINGS IN THE NATIONAL AMATEUR

IN 1910, the national amateur championship was awarded to the Country Club, and I made up my mind to play in that tournament. I was still in high school and playing interscholastic golf. The schoolboys were to have their championship at the Woodland Golf Club. I played more golf at Woodland than at any other course and I looked forward to the event. Winning the qualifying medal with a 77 I met my school companion, Francis Mahan, in the second round and though I scored a 77, which was fine golf for the class of competition, I was soundly beaten by three up and two to play. Mahan made the amazing score of 73, a figure close to the record of the course. Francis was beaten in the next round and the championship was won by Arthur Knight of Worcester.

To compete in the national amateur championship I had to belong to a recognized golf club. My good friend Foggy Ainsworth was a member of Woodland and I asked him about the dues. He told me I could join as a junior member for twenty-five dollars. The dues for a regular member were fifty. Directly following the inter-

scholastic tournament, I put in an application
for junior membership in the Woodland Golf
Club.

When I arrived home that night I told my
mother what I had done, and she was furious. I
told her what the membership would cost and she
said, 'I suppose you have the twenty-five dollars.'
I had to say 'No' to this. She then asked where I
thought I was going to get it. I told her if she
would lend me the money, I would work that summer and repay her. Mother most reluctantly gave
in, insisting that I had to pay it back and closing
her remarks with the words that, she was 'certain
the game of golf would ruin me.'

I was elected to membership in Woodland, paid
the dues, and then got busy to find myself a job.
It was summer and vacation season. I went to
Boston day after day, trying to find something to
do that would get me sufficient money to pay my
obligation. I searched everywhere.

A week passed by and nothing turned up. Sunday morning came along, and in going through one
of the Boston papers, I noticed an advertisement
which stated that one of the leading drygoods
houses was looking for a boy. I hurried to Boston
early Monday morning and arrived at the business
establishment at seven-thirty. There wasn't a soul
around, and I had to wait outside. After perhaps
ten minutes, a fine-looking man came along and

asked me what I was doing there so early. I told him I had come to apply for the position that the firm had advertised for and showed him the clipping. He invited me in and, after answering a few perfunctory questions, I got the job.

Within five minutes the place was filled with boys, but I had landed the only open place. Mr. Mahoney was my chief, the man who let me in and signed me up, and he was the kindliest fellow in the world. I was paid the munificent sum of four dollars a week, and my duties consisted of watching the stock of bed linens and pillow slips, keeping them in orderly condition and carrying them to the shipping room. I worked for ten long weeks to save money enough to pay off my debt to Mother. Carfares and lunches made it a mighty task, but I succeeded.

I played little golf that summer. The firm had a baseball team, and I was invited to try for it. I was fond of baseball. I went out for the ball team and was selected to play first base. I cannot say much about my baseball ability, but I think I was as good as the other members of our team. I can remember one game we had. It was at the old Columbus Avenue playground.

The first time I came to bat, I caught hold of an out curve and bounded the ball off a recreation house in deep right field. It came back to the right fielder, but I made two bases on the hit. The next

25

time up I poled one against the concrete wall, well over the left fielder's head. I was thrown out at home. The third time up I connected again with the wall in left field, and once again I was thrown out trying to stretch the hit into a home run. In each case I made a desperate slide for the home plate, but the ball was there ahead of me. The diamond was of the skinned variety, and I wish you could have seen my legs. The cinders and gravel removed practically all the skin I had. My poor mother was distracted.

September first came along, and I resigned my job, because I had to go back to school and, what was more important to me, I had to get some golfing practice for the national amateur championship. My entry had to go in. All entries were sent through the club secretary, who in turn forwarded them to the United States Golf Association for acceptance. I called up the Woodland Golf Club, and told them I desired to enter the championship. Harold Tripp was secretary of the club, but no one knew where he was. I had three days in which to get my entry in, and I spent the greater part of one of these trying to reach Harold Tripp. I finally discovered he was at his summer home at Harwichport, Massachusetts, well down on Cape Cod.

I wrote Harold Tripp a letter, sent it special delivery with a money order for five dollars, and urged him to send it post-haste to New York. Then came the suspense. I wondered whether my name got in on time to be accepted. I never knew until the pairings were announced, and sure enough I was in. In 1910 there was no eligibility list and anybody could enter if he belonged to a club. My handicap at Woodland was six, and there were many higher handicapped men than I. As a result, the event attracted a tremendous number of players.

My qualifying partner was John Shepard, Jr., then at the head of a big Providence department store. We were drawn to start around three-thirty-five in the afternoon of a late September day. After playing two holes quietly, we arrived on the third tee and had to wait just one hour before playing that hole. In the tangle or congestion was the champion Bob Gardner. Some pair ahead had lost a ball and tied up the whole affair. It was slow going, and Mr. Shepard and I were forced to stop, after playing fourteen holes, on account of darkness. We returned to the clubhouse and were advised that we were to report in the morning and be on the fifteenth tee at seven o'clock. I lived close to the club, so it was no particular hardship for me to keep the appointment. Furthermore, I had played rather well and stood an excellent chance of breaking 80. Ordinary golf on those last four holes would give me 80. Mr. Shepard was not so fortunate. He decided to retire, and I was introduced to W. R. Thurston, who was in the same fix as myself in that he had to play the last four holes to complete his first round of eighteen.

The dew was still on the grass as we teed up. There was plenty of dew in my eyes, too, because I went to pieces, finished badly, and the best I could get was an 83. Twenty minutes later, I was on the first tee to start my second round, this time with Robert Watson. I played satisfactorily for nine holes, but the pangs of hunger — I had had my breakfast at six o'clock that morning — weakened me so I could hardly swing my club, and I totaled 86. My two rounds were 169, and I failed by one stroke of qualifying in my first National Amateur Championship. Bob Gardner also failed by one stroke, and there were many good ones left out.

With the strain out of the way, I enjoyed the week immensely and watched all the great golfers in action. Chick Evans was coming strong and had caught the fancy of the Brookline galleries. Fred Herreshoff was another. I saw Chick Evans lose his semi-final match to Bill Fownes after being two up and three to play. Fownes won the last three holes due to brilliant play on his part and a complete collapse on the part of Evans on the putting greens. You can learn much by observation and I gained many a fine lesson watching the stars. The final was played between Warren Wood and Bill Fownes.

Fownes was too steady through the fairways and too deadly on the putting greens for the more erratic Warren, and won by four up and three to play.

Three weeks later came the annual Country Club tournament. This event ranked next in importance to the state amateur championship. Golfers came from all parts of the country to compete, and it was a blue-ribbon affair, one sought after by everyone, including myself. To win the Country Club Cup was a real accomplishment. A qualifying round was held, and the sixteen low scorers survived for the match-play test. I played my round in the morning and made a 76, which score, if I do say so, was really good.

P. W. Whittemore, known to his friends as 'Buck,' equaled my total and we led the field, tying for the medal prize. My first-round opponent was Ray Gorton, the fellow who did so well against Bobby Jones in the national amateur championship in 1928. Gorton has always been a fine golfer, and in the 1910 championship he qualified easily and won a match or two before he was beaten. Therefore, I was up against it in my first match-play round in the Country Club Cup Tournament. I started none too confidently, but after a few holes I found I was holding my own, the nervousness had worn off, and I set myself for the battle. At the end of the fourteenth hole we stood even. Then a peculiar thing happened.

A Game of Golf

I had the honor and hit a fine ball down the middle of the fairway. We had the wind behind us. Ordinarily a long tee shot would stop just short of the road, and from there it was an easy mashie shot to a well-trapped green. I was quite pleased with my drive. Gorton followed suit with another that was perfect in every respect. His ball carried almost to the road and with a long bound seemed certain to roll well beyond. At about the same moment his ball landed, an automobile was entering the grounds, and just as Ray's ball was crossing the driveway, it came in contact with the radiator of the fast-moving machine, with a result that it was directed off course and driven yards from where it should have been into the bushes around the clubhouse. It was one of the most unfortunate things I have ever seen and a most undeserved fate for a fine drive.

My own ball had come to rest in the middle of the road among some loose stones which ordinarily would have been a severe penalty, but under the circumstances it was nothing to what Gorton suffered. I can still see the expression of surprise on the face of Ray as he was told what had happened to his ball. It was a rub of the green and he had to play the ball out of the bushes. He barely got it out onto the lawn in front of the clubhouse. A long iron carried his ball over the traps guarding the green, and as though the fates were still leveled dead against him, it got a mean bound and rolled over the green and under a low-branched beech tree. That was his third, and I had not played my second.

My ball in the road was not lying too badly, but I figured Ray must take at least a six for the hole and I did not care to risk getting into the trap near the green. Consequently, I played a safe shot from the road. Then I approached not too well, but succeeded in reaching the green twenty-five feet from the hole on my third. Ray played a marvelous stroke from under the tree eight feet from the cup. I was now playing the like and I putted four feet short. Ray holed his eight-footer for a five; I missed mine and lost a hole that a minute or two before seemed a cinch to win. To make a long story short, I was beaten by Ray two and one, and to this day I have never deliberately played a shot safely if there was any possible chance of getting it away. On the theory that there is no such thing as a safe stroke in golf, I prefer to take any reasonable risk, and this policy has helped me win many matches.

I forget whether Buck Whittemore withdrew from match play or was beaten, but in any event we got together to play off our tie for the medal. In my home I have a handsome silver tray with this inscription on it:

A Game of Golf

The Country Club
Oct. 13th 1910
Best Gross
Won by
F. Ouimet

This trophy is a souvenir that reminds me of an extremely amusing incident that happened during our play-off, although it was anything but amusing at the time. Whenever Buck Whittemore and I get together, we laugh about that game, and I really suppose I should present the tray to Buck as a balm or something.

Buck Whittemore was a great golfer and he still plays as well as ever. In 1910, he was rated one of the best golfers in the East. At the end of the first nine holes, he had a two-stroke advantage over me, our scores reading 39 and 41. Thirty-nine was fine going. The tenth hole was a short one, about a hundred and thirty-five yards. Buck pitched clear over the green into the rough beyond. I got on. As I stood in back of my ball, I studied the territory as I waited for Buck to play. I figured Buck would take at least a four, and the three I hoped to get would reduce his lead a stroke. Then it occurred to me that Buck had not found his ball, so I started to help him in his search. He himself discovered it. I stood aside, as Buck took his stance. I saw him slap his leg. Then his arm. After that his forehead. Presently a swarm of bees completely surrounded him and stung him all over. He beat a hasty retreat from the spot as the bees followed. He asked me what he should do.

'Drop one as near as possible to the spot where your ball lies,' I said. Buck informed me he was not going to return anywhere near the 'spot' and if it was satisfactory, he would drop a ball in a safer place. I agreed. Buck's fingers had swelled up so much he could hardly grip his club. He holed out in five and I evened the score. From there in, Buck could do nothing. The countless stings took his mind off the game and every stroke he made was agonizing. Needless to say, I won the play-off and the prize bears mute proof to an exciting day.

About that time further improvements were made in the golf ball. Smaller and heavier ones were in fashion and they could be hit yards farther than the larger and lighter ones. They putted better, too, and the scoring began to improve as a consequence. A ball came across from England that was not only smaller and heavier, but had an acid center. This ball, hard to obtain, was called the Zodiac. It was very long. Caddie boys had a habit of cutting the Zodiacs open and several had bad accidents as a result.

In the spring of 1911, I entered the thirty-six-hole medal-play tournament of the Woodland Golf Club. It was open to all amateur golfers and a large field entered. The best score I had ever been able to make at Woodland was 74. In the morning, the first day, I swept well into the lead by making a record of 70 — 36 out and 34 home. It was an unusually low score in competition and many, including myself, wondered how high I should 'blow' the following day. I got going in my second round precisely as I had in the round of 70, almost hole for hole. With the exception of one slip coming home, there was absolutely no difference in the two scores, the 70 the first round and the 71 on the second. Playing two consecutive rounds such as these had more to do with steadying my game than any other thing and helped me to win several minor events.

That summer of 1911 I had developed a friendship with Heinrich Schmidt, of Worcester, and it was give and take between us, although Heinie seemed to have the better of me in the more important competitions. We qualified in the state amateur championship at Essex County, and met in the second round. While waiting on a tee, we began talking of our ambitions in golf. Heinie said, 'It is my ambition to win the state amateur championship.' I smiled and said, 'Heinie, it is my ambition to win the national amateur championship.' This provoked a bit of mirth on the part of Schmidt, who thought I should point toward something within my reach.

In any event Heinie knocked me out on that day.

34

The next year he beat me in the finals of the state amateur championship, and thus achieved his ambition. I competed in the national amateur events in both 1911 and 1912, and each time failed by a single stroke to qualify. I shall never forget my experience in the championship of 1911. My partner was Chick Evans, and it was a rare treat for an eighteen-year-old boy to have the opportunity of playing with such a bright star whose game had caught the fancy of the American golfing public.

I was so impressed with the play of Evans, I suppose I did not or could not concentrate as seriously as I should have done. My putting, too, was terrible, and on one green I required four putts from a short distance. The experience of playing with Evans was extremely helpful, and he encouraged me greatly as we played along together, each little realizing that some day we were to become serious rivals on the golf course.

I have already called attention to the fact that Heinrich Schmidt realized a boyhood ambition in winning the state amateur title in 1912. We came together in the final round. Heinie had earned the reputation of being a very slow player. I do not think it was because he played so slowly, but rather because he was exceedingly careful. He left nothing to chance and weighed each situation deliberately. He never wasted a stroke through carelessness. Withal he was a splendid match player.

35

It has always been my nature to do things quickly. On the golf course in matches, it was a habit of mine to decide matters instantly and try to put them into execution. Against Schmidt I planned a different method of procedure. I knew he would take time studying his shots, so I decided to do the same thing. Whether the change from more natural methods upset my play or not, I cannot say, but I do know I got off on the wrong foot and struggled all morning long against a methodical opponent who cashed in on each of my mistakes.

Late in the afternoon, with the match almost beyond reach, I changed my careful tactics and simply hit my ball as was my custom. Dormie four down, I won the fifteenth and sixteenth holes. Playing the short seventeenth, I missed the green badly. Heinie was on. I approached inside his ball, but I was still ten feet from the hole after playing two. His approach putt left him a four-footer for a three. I holed my ten-footer, and when he missed, I won the hole and was now only one down, with one to play. I had taken three holes in a row.

Playing the eighteenth, I had by far the better of the play and was in a splendid position to square the match. My second shot had left my ball a few feet off the edge of the green. All I had to do was to chip close. Somewhat excited and overanxious, I

36

took three practice shots within a few inches of the ball. I did not play a good chip and was left with a six-foot putt for my four. Heinie had taken five. Henry Wilder was the referee. I did my best to sink the six-footer, but failed. Then Wilder informed me that I had taken three extra strokes because there was a penalty for each of the practice swings I had taken within a club's length of the ball. It was true, and Wilder had no alternative. I have often felt that it was a fine thing I missed my putt because it relieved the situation perfectly for everybody. As it was, Schmidt was the winner by two holes.

CHAPTER III

THE OPEN CHAMPIONSHIP OF 1913

NINETEEN-THIRTEEN was a big year, and the state championship played no small part. To begin with, I had a nineteen-hole match with Brice Evans. Then I was three down and five to play against Ray Gorton. Playing the eighteenth hole I was one down. We both reached the green on our seconds to the last hole at Wollaston, where the event was played. I got down in two putts and was on the point of conceding an eighteen-inch putt to Ray, which meant the match, when something prompted me to refrain from doing so. I stepped aside ready to grasp his hand the moment he holed the putt. To my amazement he missed, and the match was even. It taught me a good lesson — that is, never to concede the putt that is to defeat you. I beat Ray on the nineteenth.

The semi-final came, and this time I was opposed to John G. Anderson who was playing the finest golf of his life. John, possibly remembering our school-day clash when I caught him off form, was bent on squaring the account. At the twelfth hole he was two up. I proceeded then to go wild. I made a two on the short thirteenth and played the next four holes in three each. It gave me the match by three up and one to play. The approach to the

38

seventeenth hole was blind, and John stood off to one side near the green to watch my ball. I knew I had hit a fine shot and looked over to where John was standing. John, with both hands in the air, said, 'Your ball is stone dead.' It was just twelve inches from the cup.

Even though beaten, John was thrilled, and asked me to play out the last hole. I made that in three also. My finish of 2–3–3–3–3–3 was six under par. My opponent in the final was Frank Hoyt, and I beat him ten up and nine to play. An interesting thing happened in Hoyt's semi-final match with Buck Whittemore. Hoyt knew Wollaston, and its many tricky approach shots, like a book. Playing the fifteenth, they stood even. Buck had driven to the right of the hole, expecting the contour of the ground to throw his ball down toward the green. He did not have quite enough length, and his ball stopped above the green, leaving him a difficult short approach to lay it dead. Hoyt was on with a long tee shot. Golf tournaments in 1913 were anything but serious affairs, and everyone played the game for the sport there was in it. Buck said, 'This is a tough shot.' Hoyt agreed. Buck failed to get his ball anywhere near the hole, and Hoyt won it.

'Buck, I will bet you a dollar I can lay a ball dead from where you just played,' said Hoyt, whom we called 'Stealthy Steve.'

'You're on,' said Buck.

Hoyt dropped a ball, played far up to the right. It seemed to stop for a fraction of a second and then, rolling ever so gently, came to rest about six inches from the hole. He collected the dollar.

The next feature was the national amateur championship. Jerry Travers was defending his title at Garden City, Long Island. The usual big field gathered for the qualifying round and there was plenty of talent. I played a very steady game in the first round and finished with a score of 75, one stroke better than the next man, Walter J. Travis. I was thrilled to death because it was the first time in the amateur championship that I had played consistently. The next day I scored a 76 and my thirty-six-hole total was one better than Travis's.

Friends in the locker room congratulated me and said that I was bound to win the medal for the qualifying round. I told them I was more than satisfied to qualify and was not worrying over winning the medal. It was just as well. Chick Evans had a 77 his first round. He was 39 out and needed a 34 on the last nine to beat me for low-score honors. A 34 today is a hard assignment at Garden City, and in 1913 it seemed almost impossible. All Chick did was to breeze home in 32, and the medal was his beyond any doubt.

I won one match and was then called upon to

play the champion, Jerome D. Travers. Jerry had a terrible time on the last hole, a short one, over the pond, and the resultant seven he took on his second qualifying round almost knocked him out. As it was, he had to play off for a position in the match play rounds and I drew him after we had each won a match. To say I was overawed would be expressing it mildly: I was scared to death. Here was an opponent who had won three national championships and was conceded to be the greatest match-play exponent of the game. But there was nothing to do but to put on a bold front, and away we went.

The match was very close all morning. Holes were hard to win. Jerry seemed cold as ice. He accepted good shots with the same attitude as he did poor ones. I complimented him on his fine shots. My good ones seem to pass unnoticed. After a time I thought, this fellow is determined to do just one thing and that is to win the golf game. I made up my mind to do the same. It was a thirty-six-hole match. Playing the eighteenth — the short one — we were even. Both reached the green with Jerry inside. I placed my putt from thirty feet on the edge of the cup. Jerry took one look at me and then proceeded to sink a twenty-footer, to become one up. I have always felt he did that to impress me, and it certainly did.

When we appeared on the first tee for the last

half of the match a tremendous gallery awaited. Travers increased his lead by winning the first hole. Off and on in the morning round he drove with a driver, and he missed many tee shots, although his recoveries and putting were positively amazing. I took the second and third holes and won the seventh to become one up. The golf was almost perfect — nothing given away. Playing the eighth or twenty-sixth hole, I hit a fine tee shot. Jerry was out in front with his black driving iron. I hit a fine iron of at least a hundred and eighty yards eight feet from the cup. I was proud of that shot, and looked at Jerry as much as to say, 'There, let's see you beat that one.' He took a bit more time than usual, made his swing, met the ball, and when it stopped, it was ten inches from the cup. That took the starch out of me, and I was beaten from then on.

That match with Jerome Travers did more toward getting me into the proper frame of mind than any I had ever had. I had been inclined to look upon golf lightly. A contest meant nothing more than a trip around the course. If my golf was good enough, I should win, and if not, then there was nothing to do but congratulate the winner. I learned that one must keep his thoughts focused entirely on the shot at hand, and in a hard match it is silly to be too passive. Jerry came to me in the locker room afterward and we went over our match hole by hole. I saw in Jerry Travers a great sportsman, one who put his heart and soul into the golf game, and when it was finished, he had time to reflect and express himself whole-heartedly on the simplest things.

In that same championship a funny thing happened in the match between Eben Byers and Chick Evans. Chick held a commanding lead for the better part of twenty-seven holes; then Byers began pecking away, winning a hole here and there, until they reached the home one. Evans was one up. Both got on the green. Chick was putting poorly as usual, but when he coasted an approach putt up to within three feet of the hole, it looked like a certain victory. Byers putted, got just inside Evans's ball and stymied him. Chick tried to jump the stymie, but failed, and his ball ran two feet beyond the cup. Byers putted again, missed, and again stymied Chick. Once more Chick missed and lost the hole. He was hard put to it to win on the thirty-ninth green.

Chick figured in another distressing situation. Against John Anderson in the semi-final round, he had been having a dreadful time of it on the greens. His tee shots were perfect and his irons sparkled with effectiveness, but his putting was woeful. He carried four putters in his bag and after so many sad experiences each had plenty to do. He never got acquainted with any one of them because he was shifting from one to another on every green. Finally, left with a three-foot putt to keep the match alive, he was at a loss to know which putter to use. He picked one out of his bag. He put it back and handled another. He tried them all, and the one he eventually selected was the wrong one.

The President of the United States Golf Association in 1913 was none other than Robert Watson, the man I had played with in my second qualifying round four years previously at the Country Club. The open championship was to be played at the Country Club, and Watson was seeking a good amateur entry. He thought I should enter. I argued with him about the folly of such a thing, and he won the argument. I was through school and employed by Wright and Ditson in the sporting goods business. I had taken my vacation by going to Garden City for the national amateur championship and I did not have the courage to ask for more time off to play in the Open.

Returning to Boston, I settled down to work. Vardon and Ray had come to this country to give golf exhibitions and also to play in the Open. One morning the papers carried the pairings for the open championship, and my chief came to me and said, 'Well, I see you are now going to play in the open championship.' John Morrill was an executive in Wright and Ditson's and a kindlier or more lovable character never lived. I might say the same about George Wright, who did as much toward developing the game of golf in this country as any man.

I was embarrassed. I told Mr. Morrill I had no intention of playing, but if he would be good enough to let me wander out to Brookline and see Vardon and Ray perform, I should be ever grateful to him. With a gleam in his eye, he said, 'As long as you have entered, you had better plan to play.' This was an order. I needed no further instructions.

The Sunday before the open tournament, I played at the Wellesley Country Club with friends. I bring this up merely to show you that one's form in golf is a mercurial affair. With the open championship two days away, I made two scores of 88 on a short and rather easy nine-hole course, the 88's being just twenty-two strokes higher than a record score I had established on one of my earlier rounds over the layout. The friend who invited me to play with himself and friends was broken-hearted, and thought he had ruined my game. I told him not to worry; that I had probably got all the bad golf out of my system — and, believe me, there must have been plenty of it in there. There was such a huge entry the field was divided into three qualifying sections and I was in the same group with Harry Vardon. With a 74 in my morning round, I finished a stroke ahead of Vardon. That was an accomplishment. In the afternoon I was playing quite

45

as well until I reached the long fourteenth, and bumping into much trouble, I made a seven. At that I scored a 78 which ranked me next to Vardon, the leader in our section.

There is little to be said about the championship itself. After the first three rounds, I was tied with both Vardon and Ray at 225. Ray was finishing his final round as I walked to the first tee. I watched him hole out and learned he had made a 79. It was raining, but, even so, a 79 did not seem very low. It made his seventy-two-hole total 304. Playing the fifth hole, I was told that Vardon had tied Ray. The rumors in championship play, particularly if you happen to be in the running, come thick and fast. I was next told Barnes had the championship in the hollow of his hand. Then word came to me that Barnes had blown up.

I was having my own troubles out in that rain and nothing would go right. Out in 43, all hope seemed gone. Then someone said, 'Tellier will win in a walk.' The tenth hole was a par three. Owing to the sodden condition of the putting green, a high pitch was dangerous, because the ball would become embedded in the soft turf. I elected to use a jigger, intending to hit a low shot to the green. I forgot to look at the ball and hit it about fifteen feet. I put my next on the green eight feet from the hole and then took three putts for an inglorious five. Then I learned that Tellier had got into trouble and had finished behind both Vardon and Ray, who were still leading.

After that wretched five, walking to the eleventh tee between a lane of spectators, I heard one man say, 'It's too bad, he has blown up.' I knew he meant me, and it made me angry. It put me in the proper frame of mind to carry on. There was still a chance, I thought. People lined the fairway as I drove. A par four was helpful on the eleventh. A hard five on the twelfth helped not at all, because here was a hole where one might be expected to save a stroke, although it was a difficult four. Standing on the thirteenth tee, I realized I must play those last six holes in two under par to tie. There were two holes on the course where I thought I might save a stroke: the thirteenth, the one I had to play next, which was a drive and a short pitch, and the sixteenth, a short hole. I selected these two holes for reasons. I had been quite successful on the thirteenth and had scored threes there regularly. I had not made a two all the week, and I had a hunch I should get one at the sixteenth. It was just a hunch.

My drive to the thirteenth was satisfactory. With a simple pitch to the green, I mishit the ball and barely escaped a trap. My ball lay off the green thirty feet from the hole I had selected as one upon which to beat par. Instead of having a reasonably short putt, I was stuck with a chip

shot. In any event, I chipped my ball right into
the hole for my three and was still in the hunt.
A routine five came on the long fourteenth. I
missed my second to the fifteenth badly, so badly,
I missed every trap. I pitched on and got my par
four.

Then came the sixteenth, the hole I had been
expecting to make in two. I not only did not get
my two there, but actually had to hole a nine-
footer for the three. One of the last two holes had
to be made in three, the other in four. They were
both testing holes. As I splashed along in the mud
and rain, I had no further hunches. I just wanted
an opportunity to putt for one of those threes. I
got it on the seventeenth. A drive and second
shot, played with a jigger placed my ball on the
green fifteen feet from the cup. It was now or
never. As I looked the line of putt over, I thought
of one thing, giving the ball a chance — that is,
getting it to the hole. I struck that putt as firmly
as any putt I ever hit, saw it take the roll, bang
smack against the back of the hole, and fall in
for the three.

Now to get the four. A drive split the fairway
to the last hole and was out far enough so that a
long iron could reach the green. Eddie Lowery,
my ten-year-old caddie, handed me an iron and
said, 'Keep your eye on the ball and hit it.' I did.
I lifted my head just in time to see the ball sail

48

toward the pin, saw it land and, as I thought, kick forward, and I can then remember saying to Eddie, 'I have a putt to win this championship.' I was certain I had seen my ball clear the embankment and hop forward. As a matter of fact, the ball struck the top of the bank, and stopped instantly just off the cut surface of the putting green. A chip shot left me a four-foot putt which I popped in. I had ended that seventy-two-hole stretch in a tie with Vardon and Ray for the championship I had been most reluctant to enter.

Friends hustled me into the locker room building and the excitement was tremendous. One individual came to me and asked this question, 'Were you bothered while putting on the seventeenth green?' 'Not a bit,' was my reply. 'Why?' He went on to say that the highway directly in back of the green was littered with automobiles, so much so that it was impossible for machines to move in either direction. Just then a motor came along, and the driver, seeing his path blocked completely, kept up a constant tooting of his horn, as I was preparing to putt. I never heard a single sound, so thoroughly was my mind centered on the business of holing the putt.

After taking a bath, I walked home and turned in early for a real night's rest. I slept from nine-thirty until eight the next morning, and after a light breakfast, hustled over to the Country Club for

49

my play-off with Vardon and Ray. I did not feel nervous or unduly excited. I slipped on my golf shoes, got hold of Eddie Lowery, and went out to the Polo Field to hit a few practice shots. There was nobody around. The shots I hit felt fine. Soon some people came along and watched me. After perhaps a half-hour's practice, I was told that Vardon and Ray were on the first tee waiting for the match to begin.

Johnny McDermott took my arm and said, 'You are hitting the ball well; now go out and pay no attention whatsoever to Vardon or Ray. Play your own game.' It was excellent advice and I promised Johnny I would do my best.

On the way to the tee my good friend Frank Hoyt (Stealthy Steve') asked me if I would not permit him to carry my clubs. I had played much golf with Steve and he was a master in the finer points of the game. I told him he must see Eddie Lowery. He made one or two offers of money, but they did not tempt Eddie in the least. It was interesting to see the reaction of Eddie as he definitely and positively refused to be bought off. Finally, Hoyt appealed to me. I looked at the ten-year-old Eddie, his eyes filled, and I think he was fearful that I would turn him down. In any event, he seemed so sincere I did not have the heart to take the clubs away from him, and my final gesture was to tell Steve, Eddie was going to caddie for me.

It was raining, and the three of us were ushered into the tent near the tee to draw lots for the honor. I drew the longest straw and had to drive first. As I walked over to the sand box, and realized what I was up against and saw the crowd, I was terribly excited. If I could only get my tee shot away! Eddie stepped up as he handed me a driver and said, 'Be sure and keep your eye on the ball.' The opening salute was a drive well down the middle of the fairway and for good length. Vardon and Ray followed suit. Ray was the only one who was long enough to reach the green on his second, but he sliced a brassie to the right.

We all got on in three and took fives on the hole. I was left with a four-foot putt for my five, and I worried not a little over it. I tapped it in, and then almost instantly any feeling of awe and excitement left me completely. I seemed to go into a coma. Eddie kept telling me to keep my eye on the ball. He cautioned me to take my time. He encouraged me in any number of different ways. My first mistake was on the fifth hole where the slimy grip turned in my hand and my second shot went out of bounds. But Vardon and Ray both erred on the same hole, and I was safe for the time being. Ray had taken a five on the third to our fours, and that was the only difference in the scores up to that point.

Vardon made the sixth in three and went into the

lead. Ray was now trailing Vardon by two strokes
and me by one. The seventh hole at Brookline is a
hard par three. Vardon was to the right of the
green with his iron and needed four. I failed to lay
a long approach putt dead, and took four. Ray
was the only one to get a three and he pulled up on
even terms with me.

The eighth hole was sensational. This hole measures three hundred and eighty yards and the view
of the green is more or less restricted by a hill. You
can see the flag, but no part of the green. We all
had fine drives. A tremendous crowd had gathered
around the green to see the balls come up. I
played my second with a mashie straight for the
pin. In a few seconds a mighty roar went up. As I
handed the club to Eddie, he said, 'Your ball is
stone dead.' I wanted to think it was, but I wished
also to prepare myself in case it was not. Therefore
I said to Eddie, 'It is not stone dead, but I believe I
shall have a putt for my three.' You see I did not
wish to be disappointed.

As we walked toward the green and came to the
top of the hill, I saw a ball twelve inches from the
hole. It was mine. Ray was forty feet away with a
sidehill putt and he tapped his ball as delicately as
possible. It took the necessary turns and rolled
right into the hole. Vardon had a four, and I got
my three, which put us all even at the end of eight
holes.

The next highlight was the short tenth. This green was so soggy that both Vardon and Ray, after pitching on, had to chip over the holes made by their balls as they bit into the soft turf and hopped back. I was fairly close in one. My opponents failed to make their threes, and I stepped into the lead by a stroke.

I added another stroke on the twelfth, where I got my four to their fives. Vardon dropped a nice putt for a three on the thirteenth, one under par, which brought him within a stroke of me. The long fourteenth was important. Ray might reach the green in two, but it was beyond the range of Vardon and myself. Ray drove last, and I saw him hurl himself at his ball to get just a little added length. When he played his second from the fairway, he put every bit of power into the shot, but his timing was poor and he hit the ball far to the right into a grove of chestnut trees. He recovered beautifully, and the hole was made in five by all.

I was paying as little attention as possible to the strokes of the others, because I did not wish to be unduly influenced by anything they did. I was simply carrying out McDermott's instructions and playing my own game. I could not help but notice, however, that Ray was struggling somewhat. I noticed, too, that Vardon, who seemed to be a master in mashie work, pulled his pitch to the green, which was not his natural way of playing such a stroke. Vardon normally played his pitches with a slight fade from left to right.

Ray got into all sorts of trouble on the fifteenth and he seemed out of the running. I never gave it a thought as he holed out in six. I still clung to my one stroke lead over Vardon through the sixteenth. Ray was now five strokes behind. Vardon had the honor on the seventeenth tee. This hole is a semi-dog-leg, and by driving to the right you eliminate all risk. On the other hand, if the player chooses to risk a trap on the left and gets away with it, he has a short pitch to the green. Vardon drove to the left. I saw his ball start, and that is all. I drove to the right. Ray tried to cut the trees on the left and hit a prodigious wallop that cleared everything, but his ball was in the long grass.

As we walked toward our balls, I saw that Vardon had caught the trap and his ball was so close to the bank he had no chance at all of reaching the green. He could just play out to the fairway. I knocked a jigger shot to the green, my ball stopping fifteen feet above the hole. Ray and Vardon took fives. As I studied my putt, I decided to take no liberties with the skiddy surface and simply tried to lay the ball dead for a sure four. I putted carefully and watched my ball roll quietly toward the hole. It went in for a three. With one hole left, I was now in the lead by three strokes over Vardon and seven over Ray.

54

The eighteenth hole was a hard two-shotter. The rains had turned the race-track in front of the green into a bog, and my one thought was to get over the mud. All hit fine tee shots. I placed my second on the green. It did not enter my head that I was about to become the open champion until I stroked my first putt to within eight or nine inches of the hole. Then, as I stepped up to make that short putt, I became very nervous. A veil of something that seemed to have covered me dropped from around my head and shoulders. I was in full control of my faculties for the first time since the match started, but terribly excited. I dropped the putt. Nothing but the most intense concentration brought me victory.

I was fearful at the beginning that I should blow up, and I fought against this for all I was worth. The thought of winning never entered my head, and for that reason I was immune to emotions of any sort. My objective was to play eighteen holes as well as I could and let the score stand for good or bad. I accomplished a feat that seemed so far beyond anything I ever hoped to do that, while I got a real thrill out of it, I felt I had been mighty lucky. Had I harbored the desire to win that championship or an open title of any kind, I might have been tickled beyond words. In sport one has to have the ambition to do things and that ambition in my case was to win the national ama-

teur championship.   Therefore, I honestly think
I never got the 'kick' out of winning the open
title that I might have done if I had thought I could
win it.

CHAPTER IV

ENGLISH EXPERIENCES AND THE NATIONAL AMATEUR CHAMPIONSHIP OF 1914

IN 1914 I decided to go abroad and play in the British championships. I might say now that British golf was on a very high plane and a golfer's education was not complete unless he had had the experience of playing seaside courses in the winds that prevailed.

The amateur championship was to be played at Sandwich and the open at Prestwick in Scotland. With Arthur Lockwood as a traveling companion, I sailed from Boston and landed at Dover. At the point of disembarkation we were greeted by several golf writers and a horde of photographers. After answering hundreds of questions and posing for countless pictures, Lockwood and I were permitted to go to our hotel — the Lord Walden I think it was — for a night of rest in a real bed.

I was naturally anxious to get out on a golf course after a rough and stormy trip across the water. At breakfast the next morning, I was conscious that several of the newspaper men were sitting at a table near mine. I am sure it was not their intention to embarrass me, but they watched closely what I ate for my breakfast and one of the afternoon editions of a London paper carried the information that I had grapefruit, eggs, toast and coffee for my morning meal. Arthur Lockwood and I repaired to the near-by course at Deal, and here I hit my first drive — and very poorly too — on an English championship course. Later on, I visited London, and spent a day going through the Tower of London, Westminster Abbey, and other points of historical interest.

It was difficult to play a practice round peacefully. Wherever I went a group of curious newspaper men followed. I must say my game was anything but worthy of the United States open champion, and it was hard for the English people to understand how I had happened to beat both Vardon and Ray. Lockwood originally came from a place called Weston-Super-Mare near Bristol, and since this place was more or less away from the beaten path, he thought I could get a quiet practice session on his old course.

Word of our anticipated trip to Weston-Super-Mare preceded us and flaming posters, carrying the wording, 'Boy Wonder to play at Weston,' greeted us when we arrived. Weston-Super-Mare was a great playground, a beautiful spot, and since it was about the time of the Whitsun holidays the place was filled with vacationists. Quiet practice rounds were out of the question and my golf went from bad to worse. Finally, in despair, with con-

58

fidence much shattered, Arthur suggested that we motor to Westward Ho!

This wonderful course is situated in southwestern England and is a difficult place to reach. Jerome Travers and Fred Herreshoff, two of my American friends, were at practice there, so we decided to join them. Travers had just won the Prince of Wales Medal with a grand round of 74 and was very much on his game. I began to play a little better, and since the championship was four or five weeks away, I still had the opportunity of getting into shape.

I had an engagement to play with Harold Hilton in the Golf Illustrated Gold Vase Tournament at Sunningdale. On the way to London — it was a long train ride — I sat in my compartment with my clubs and a handbag under the seat. Two English chaps entered and took seats. They evidently were golf enthusiasts and seeing my clubs began a discussion about 'The Young American.' I was reading a paper and covered my face lest they might recognize me. One said, 'The Young American' knew very little about the game and was poor indeed compared to the better English players. I sincerely enjoyed hearing all about myself. I had bought an English golf suit with the name of the London maker inside. Those clothes came in for much discussion, and my train companions had an idea it was of American manufacture. I did feel chagrined about this, because I thought I had bought the last word in English golfing attire. My golf shoes, high ones, were thought to be football shoes. I tell you I had a grand time!

It is only fair to say, however, that everywhere I went I was treated with the utmost courtesy by everyone. The American boys, Travers, Herreshoff, Fraser Hale, Harold Weber, and myself, were entered in the Gold Vase event. When the day arrived for this tournament, all but Weber and I withdrew. It was a thirty-six-hole medal-play tournament. Hilton, my partner, was at the zenith of his career, and a tremendous gallery gathered around the first tee to see us drive. The day was wet and cold. Hilton asked me to drive first.

Directly at the left of the first tee was the eighteenth green. I teed up my ball with both knees shaking, took a swing, hit my ball up near the neck of my driver, and it rolled weakly over onto the eighteenth green after traveling about twenty yards. You can imagine my feelings! It was the first time I had had an attack of nerves. I could not see the ball. A seven graced my card as a starter and I was never so thankful in my life when that day was over, having scored two 83's, which were many strokes higher than the cards of almost all the other competitors. My confidence was badly shaken, and it was now time to go to Sandwich for the championship. I played several rounds with Hilton there. The winds were too difficult for my type of iron shot, but I did observe Hilton's methods, and two days before the championship I changed completely my manner of hitting irons. Hilton had a habit of hitting crisp strokes against, and into, severe cross-winds. I noticed he kept his right thumb on top of the shaft. I tried this. I discovered it shortened my backswing tremendously and permitted me to hit the ball a smart, decisive blow. Of course I did not have sufficient time to perfect the shot, but I stuck to it, and was beaten in the second round by two holes.

In the mean time Jerry Travers, who had been selected as a warm favorite to win the title, was beaten in the first match-play round. This was one of the most complete reversals of form I have ever seen. Jerry had been playing splendidly ever since his arrival in the British Isles, but the day before the championship he had gone stale. He could do nothing right, and it was pitiful to see our amateur champion go down to defeat when his opponent, suffering from lumbago, could do no better than 88 for his round.

Chick Evans had come over unexpectedly to play in the championship, and whereas the other American contenders had six weeks or two months of preparation, Evans had given himself only three or four days to get into shape. It was no time before he began hitting the ball perfectly. He reached the fifth round. There he was opposed to a chap named C. B. MacFarlane, a well-known player. A peculiar thing happened on the very first hole in this match. Evans hit a fine long ball well across the famous undulation known as the 'Kitchen.' MacFarlane was in the Kitchen, from where he hit a long iron straight for the pin. Evans followed with a high pitch that seemed to hit at the flag. When the green was reached the two balls were close to the hole, one about two feet, away the other four. The one nearest the hole was MacFarlane's and it was dead in the way of Evans's. Chick failed to negotiate the stymie, and then those of us watching the match were treated to one of the most bizarre stretches of golf we had ever seen. On the tough, windswept Sandwich course, with a six on the par four fourth, MacFarlane was out in 31 and stood five up. He holed several long putts, two chip shots, and could do nothing wrong. Evans played well enough to beat anybody in the field, but could not match such golf. To his credit, after being dormie six down, he won three straight holes to keep the match going. He eventually went out on the sixteenth green.

My trip to England in 1914 was a horrible failure from the competitive point of view, but that one lesson I learned from Hilton was worth all the heartaches I ever suffered.

I practiced diligently with the new iron shot, got it down fairly well in time for the open championship at Midlothian, where I was defending my title. After qualifying, I started away with a 69. I was proud of that round, because I knew it would place me at or near the top. I could not look back and pick out a single shot that I would have played over again. As I walked to the score board, the first thing that caught my eye was a score of 68. Glancing across the sheet to see its owner, I found the name of Walter Hagen. Hagen led the field from start to finish, though Chick Evans finished with two great rounds, one stroke away from Hagen.

I did not successfully defend my open championship title, but I played well enough to finish in a three-cornered tie for fourth place with Mike Brady and Jimmy Donaldson, both professionals. And finishing in a tie for fourth place was satisfying, because I had always viewed my victory of 1913 in the light of a huge fluke. My record in 1914, apart from the dismal failure in the British amateur championship, was fair. The lesson learned in playing with Harold Hilton was beginning to show results. I had crossed the English Channel, and won the amateur championship of France, had played decently in the United States open, and succeeded in winning the Massachusetts amateur event for the second time at Brae-Burn.

In connection with this tournament, I had an experience that I shall never forget. I was defending my title in 1914 as Massachusetts amateur champion and was anxious to retain it because of my play abroad. My confidence had returned and my iron shots had improved immeasurably, or at least I thought so.

In one of my match-play rounds I had a game that I can never forget and it taught me the lesson that a match is never won until it is definitely over. In the second round I was drawn against W. C. Chick, a fine golfer who played on his college team at Harvard with H. Chandler Egan. Chick devoted little time to golf but he was always prepared to put up a battle. I knew this, and as a consequence I did not take the match lightly. Things broke favorably for me, and at the end of nine holes I stood four up. I added one more hole to this rather comfortable lead and, standing on the thirteenth tee, was five up and six to play.

Then the fun started. We both reached the thirteenth green with an iron. I was away, and on my approach putt I putted too firmly and my ball rolled eight feet past the cup. Chick putted close and when I failed to sink my putt for the three, I lost the hole.

On the fourteenth I took three putts again from a long distance and lost that hole also. Now with three up and four to go, the match did not bother me particularly, because, while I had required three putts on two successive greens, at the same time they were difficult ones to lay dead and there was a real excuse for losing them. I was somewhat worried when Chick placed a fine pitch close to the cup on the fifteenth, to win with a three. Two up and three, I felt it was time to call a halt and stop Chick's surge if possible.

The sixteenth hole was a hard two-shotter. For the second, after a well-hit drive, the player is left with a blind shot. We both reached the green in two, and to my chagrin Chick holed a long putt for another three, to reduce my lead to a single hole. I was very nervous. It is a miserable sensation to have a match well in hand and then lose four holes in a row. The seventeenth was one of those hard one-shotters. Chick reached the green, on the left-hand corner, with a splendid spoon shot. With the exception of those two greens, where I needed three putts, my game was sound. Choosing a cleek, I banged my ball on a line for the flag and it came to rest well on the green about fifteen feet from the hole. When we came to the cut surface, I noticed Chick had left himself with a long approach putt the start of which had to send his ball up and down a severe undulation. Further, there was quite a roll which had to be negotiated. I had every reason to think he would do well to lay his putt dead, and in the event of

my missing my own putt for a two, I should go to
the last tee with a slender lead of one up. Chick
took plenty of time and then hit his ball. It took
the undulation beautifully, and then the roll. As
it neared the hole, I knew it was going to be close.
It made another little turn and rolled as smoothly
as you please right into the cup for a two. I missed,
and had lost my fifth straight hole. The match
was square, and it was a far different situation
from being five up and six to play.

As I stood on the eighteenth tee ready to drive,
I was thinking of a dozen things. The hole was a
hard par four. We both hit good drives. Chick
missed the green with his second, and I got on.
He chipped four feet from the hole and I putted
three feet short. As I recall, I waited for Chick
to putt, expecting him to sink his ball for the four,
and I worried myself into a frenzy wondering how
I could summon enough courage to drop my three-
footer. Perhaps the strain was beginning to tell
on Chick, for he putted and missed. I tapped my
ball into the cup and won the match by one hole.

We reached the locker room and Chick said,
'I want to have a chat with you.' I sat down.
Then he opened up on me. He had had many more
years of experience at the game than I. 'You
have learned a grand lesson; that is, never let up
on an opponent.' I told him I did not let up on
him; that his brilliant play had swept me off my

feet. We reviewed the match and Chick had the feeling that I took the game a bit too carelessly after having a seemingly impregnable lead. He was wrong, although his advice was sound, because I did my best to get the match over with as quickly as possible. However, he was right to the extent that one should not take chances no matter how secure a position he may be in. Whether or not I took the match in a light vein, I can say here that it is best to win any golf game as quickly as possible and preclude a wild rush on the part of an opponent. After that experience I was on edge, and eventually won the championship.

The next matter of importance in the year 1914 was the national amateur championship. It was to be held at the Ekwanok Country Club, Manchester, Vermont. Two years before I had spent a delightful golfing holiday at Manchester and I loved the course. Situated as it is in the Green Mountains, it is a picturesque setting and a great golf layout. Jerome Travers, who had been abroad with me, was the defending champion and every player of note was entered. Chick Evans, Fred Herreshoff, Walter J. Travis were some of the contestants.

That was the year Jesse Guilford astounded the golfing world by his prodigious hitting. On the first hole there was a cross-bunker two hundred and eighty yards from the tee. The tee was somewhat elevated, which may have foreshortened the

distance somewhat, but the fact remains that
Guilford actually hit a ball that carried the bunker.
This exhibition was but one of several that earned
for him the sobriquet of 'Siege Gun.'

I needed a rest after my severe campaigning in
England, Chicago, and Massachusetts, and never
went near a golf course for ten days prior to the
amateur championship. I had lost my open title,
and was desirous of winning the amateur event.
The qualifying round ended in a tie between Bill
Fownes and Ray Gorton, with thirty-six hole totals
of 144. I came next with 145. Ray Gorton and
I lived with Fred Martin at his home, and we spent
many an interesting evening discussing the doings
of the day. Fred, who has passed on to his reward,
was the most charming host imaginable and referred to Gorton and myself as 'his stable.' We
had a great time, and all three of us qualified.

Fred was beaten in the first round. Two thirds
of 'his stable' got through the two eighteen-hole
match-play rounds, but one of his horses had a
tough time surviving the opening match. That was
me! My opponent was Max Marston. We had a
hard match, and for thirteen holes there was little
to show for our efforts because we stood square.
Then the fun started. Max hit a great tee shot
over the gravel pit in front of the fourteenth tee,
a few yards short of a trap guarding the green.
His drive must have been close to the three-

hundred-yard mark. I tried to follow suit, but overlooked the most important thing of keeping my eye on the ball, with the result that I topped ignominiously into the gravel pit a few yards below the tee. The ball came to rest under a birch tree that prevented my playing toward the hole.

The only escape was to one side, and I managed to reach the fairway with a recovery shot, but I was still a hundred and sixty yards from the green and playing three, whereas Max was lying one. I put my third shot on the green fifteen feet from the hole. Then Max played. He did not have a difficult approach to make, but in the act of lobbing his ball over the trap he picked it a trifle too clean and his ball skittered to the back edge. He putted four feet from the cup, and we both lay even in the matter of strokes played.

As I studied my putt, I thought to myself that, if I could drop the ball into the hole after my terrible tee shot, it might give me a psychological advantage. It is disturbing to have a hole as good as won and then find yourself left with a curling four-foot putt for a half. I did sink my fifteen-footer and Max did miss his, and a hole that seemed irretrievably lost was actually won. It was the last hole that was won, the remaining four being halved, and I was victor by one hole.

Now to get back to our dormitory. It was the evening before the third-round matches. Gorton and I were still in the running for the championship. He had to meet Bill Fownes next day and my opponent was Robert Gardner, the 1909 champion. We discussed everything that had taken place during the day. Finally the discussion centered about the stymie. Gorton listened attentively to the remarks, and finally said: 'Well, if anybody ever laid me a stymie, I would not know what to do, because I have never attempted to negotiate one.' With this statement we turned in to bed.

Robert Gardner had played little golf that summer and when we got together, he was so shy of practice that I won my match rather easily. With Gorton it was far different. He and Fownes had a tremendous game. There was little to choose between the pair as they battled away. Fownes finally won a hole and, standing on the eighteenth tee, the thirty-sixth of the match, he was one up. He missed the green with his second shot and Gorton was nicely home in two. From the rough Fownes pitched up, and his ball rolled well beyond. All Ray had to do apparently was to run his approach putt from twenty-five feet close to square the match. He made an excellent putt and his ball came to rest two and a half feet from the hole. A huge crowd gathered around the green, because it was the last match on the course and intensely exciting. Bill took his stance and putted. His ball rolled toward the cup, but stopped a few inches short and directly in the path of Ray's ball. If ever there was such a thing as a dead stymie, it was this. Gorton has a rare sense of humor and looked quizzically toward Fownes. He was confused for just a moment. There was no way of getting his ball into the hole without jumping the other. Selecting a mashie niblick, he tried a preliminary swing or two. Then, casting another glance at Bill, he said, 'This is going to be good, Bill; I have never tried one of these in my life.' The gallery giggled, and it was a most amusing situation, no one enjoying the predicament more than Ray, who is nothing if not a great sportsman. He pulled himself together for the effort that was to mean so much. With a gentle stroke he hit his ball smoothly. It cleared the obstacle as neatly as possible and landed in the hole on the fly, and what is more stayed there, and the match was even.

On to the thirty-seventh traveled the two. Ray pulled his tee shot and failed to get home in two. Fownes was nicely on. Ray played his approach, his third, twenty-odd feet from the cup. Bill putted to within inches of the objective, and once again his ball stopped directly in the way of his opponent's. Ray smiled as he said, 'Well, Bill, you need not worry; I can't jump this one.' He didn't.

I was now the sole remaining entry in the Martin stable. That night, before putting out the lights we had our usual confab. This time it seemed to be the consensus of opinion that Gorton had succeeded in wearing down Fownes to such an extent that I should experience little trouble in beating him. It was one of the semi-final matches, the other being that between Walter J. Travis and Jerome Travers. I met the 'weakened' Fownes in the morning, and was treated to the surprise of seeing him outdrive me consistently from every tee.

It was a brilliant match, one of the finest I have ever played, and the golf was splendid. Three times I holed long putts for twos, and on each one got nothing better than a half. It seemed I could not shake Fownes off my back. Playing the thirty-fifth hole, I was one down. Bill missed his approach to the green and I squared the match. We reached the middle of the fairway with two accurate tee shots to the home hole. For once I had outdriven Fownes and he had to play his second before me. He shoved his ball to the right of the green in the rough and the situation took on a brighter hue for me. As I came to my ball, I noticed that it was not lying well, and the distance called for a wooden club. I had seen Chick Evans in his first-round match top his second into the ditch and lose to Eben Byers. I was afraid of doing the same thing. My caddie Arthur Reed had a brassie which he passed to me. I called his attention to the lie, which was mighty close. 'Don't you think it is dangerous to play a brassie from that lie, Arthur?' I said. 'You can't get home with anything else,' was his reply. I wanted to have Arthur's assurance if for no other reason than to bolster my confidence, and here were we at loggerheads as to the club to use. I depend upon my caddie, if he is a good one, to furnish me with information that helps my confidence, and Arthur was a fine caddie. I wanted to use my cleek, which was well lofted, because I thought I could snip the ball out of the tight lie more safely than I could with a brassie. I said to Arthur,' I think I can get home with my cleek.' He came back, 'You will have to hit a tremendous cleek shot to reach that green.' That was all I wanted him to say. 'Give me that cleek.' He did, and I never hit a ball so hard in my life. I got hold of it perfectly and solidly and the ball came out of the cuppy lie and sped a few yards off the ground for the green. I could not tell whether or not I got on, because I could not see the green, but when I walked up the incline there was my ball beyond the flag and nicely on the putting surface. That placed me in a most advantageous position.

From the rough Fownes chipped on some fifteen feet from the hole. I putted close, and the issue was now squarely up to Bill to hole his long putt or lose the match. He had been dropping putts from all corners of the green, and when he hit his

ball with that smooth and deadly putting stroke'
I was sure it was going in. It lost some speed near
the hole, but it appeared to have legs enough.
Just as it was ready to topple in, it stopped right
on the brink. It looked as though its own weight
must carry it over the edge of the hole rim. But
stop it certainly did. I tapped my ball in for a winning four, and the match ended. I had reached
the final round at last, and my opponent was none
other than the great Jerry Travers.

Travers was the outstanding match player in the
country, and I must confess I was not confident
of the outcome. There was only one way to beat
him and that was to outplay him, because Jerry
gave nothing away. I thought I might have some
advantage from the tees owing to the fact that my
driving had been steady throughout previous
matches. But driving does not win championships,
and I had seen enough of Travers's golf to know
he was a deadly fellow on and around the greens.

He had forsaken his iron and was driving with
wood. We started our match without incident.
On the third green I took three putts from a rather
short distance and passed up an opportunity. On
the fifth I missed another shortish putt. Up to the
greens I was playing splendidly, but was losing
chances to win holes because of downright poor
putting. Along about the twelfth hole, with my
putting still in a state of collapse, I discovered I

was not looking at the ball, and from then on my putting improved.

With the improvement in my putting came a return of confidence, and after the twelfth hole I did not make a mistake. In the afternoon I piled up a lead and clung to it for dear life. When I finally stood six up with six to play, I became extremely conservative and tried only for a par three on the thirteenth which I felt would assure me the championship, the one golf title I wanted above all others. I did make a three and so did Jerry and the match ended in my favor six up and five to play. My old friend Bob Watson, President of the United States Golf Association, refereed the game. I waited for Jerry to do the customary handshaking act, but to my surprise he walked to his caddie, selected a driver from the bag, and hastened toward the fourteenth teeing ground.

I looked at Bob Watson and he looked at me. 'The match is over, is it not?' questioned Bob. 'Yes, I believe it is,' was my reply. Whereupon Bob hustled up the incline after Travers to ask him if he intended to play out the bye holes. 'Why? Is the match over?' asked Travers. 'Yes, you are beaten six and five,' said Bob Watson. I was somewhat embarrassed, as Jerry apologized sincerely for his error and his congratulations were as warm as they could possibly be.

To me it proved that, when Travers played a

game of golf, his heart and soul were in the play. He was a courageous golfer and never knew when he was beaten. He knew he was many down to me, but he was not going to stop trying; hence the fact that he forgot how the match stood, certainly a great tribute to a great and fighting sportsman.

To say I was happy would be expressing it mildly. I had achieved a boyhood ambition; had won the thing I desired more than anything else and I did not care what happened thereafter.

My golfing ambition, that of winning the national amateur championship, was achieved, and the satisfaction I got out of it was tremendous. It came, I believe, as the result of hard practice and determination. Each time I played in competition, I learned something new, and it was a matter of retaining the things that were helpful to me and discarding the methods that proved useless.

CHAPTER V

SOME GOLF, SOME SOLDIERING, AND
SOME BUSINESS

THE high spots of 1915 were the two national championships, the amateur and the open. The open came first and was played at Baltusrol. It was here that Jerome Travers won. Open championships had been much sought after by the amateur delegation ever since my success in 1913. In 1914, Chick Evans, after rather a slow start at Midlothian, came down the home stretch like a thoroughbred and almost caught up with Walter Hagen, failing by one stroke to tie him. Travers had established a remarkable record as a match player, but had been given little consideration in medal-play events. Shorn of his amateur title, Jerry wanted to win the open, the only tournament of major importance he had not won.

There were no Sarazens, Farrells, Joneses, Von Elms, or Burkes in 1915, but there were many great players, nevertheless, for Hagen, McNamara, Brady, MacFarlane, Evans, Hutchison, McDonald, were golfers capable of playing as well as anybody. At the end of the first thirty-six holes, Travers was very much in the running with a total of 148, two strokes behind the leaders, Jim Barnes and Louis

77

Tellier. At that his chances were not taken too seriously. When he scored a 73 on his third round, his stock went up tremendously, and he was considered a real threat. One by one the leaders fell by the wayside, and Tom McNamara, finishing with a 72 hole total of 298, loomed as the winner.

Travers had to play the last nine holes in one under par to win, and, since the last nine holes at Baltusrol were extremely difficult, it appeared to be an impossible stunt. The tenth hole was slightly over three hundred yards in length, calling for a drive and pitch to a green surrounded by water.

It was one of those holes where threes are picked up frequently, but sixes and sevens were also quite common. Travers could waste no strokes and hope to win. Therefore, he chose his driving iron for the tee shot, because it could get him far enough along for the short pitch, and he probably felt a bit more secure with this club. Then something went wrong. Instead of poking a nice straight shot down the fairway, he sliced out of bounds. He could ill-afford to do such a thing. His next shot was pulled to the rough. It seemed as though the pressure was beginning to tell, but Jerry Travers was one of those rare athletes who do their best under trying circumstances. From the rough he pitched beautifully over the water and his ball stopped two feet from the hole. He had retrieved the stroke lost on the out-of-bounds shot, because the penalty then for such a mistake was loss of distance only.

The eleventh hole was equally exciting. A good drive left the player with a comfortable mashie to an elevated green. Jerry topped his ball with a driver, miserably, and the long grass in front of the tee quickly smothered his ball. He was no more than forty yards out and in the rough. With his mashie he knocked his ball along up the fairway. Then another mashie shot put him on the green thirty-five feet above the cup. He had to hole that putt for his par four, and that is exactly what he did. Here were two holes in succession where he had pulled himself together after two terrible mistakes, a true test of a champion. The next two holes were played in par figures and he came to the fifteenth.

This was a par five hole, but one of those that could be reached in two. It measured slightly over four hundred and fifty yards. There was no particular problem to the tee shot, because the fairway is wide and offers plenty of latitude for the ball that was hit off line. Jerry hit a good drive. He could get home with a brassie, but there was a deep trap fifty or sixty yards from the green that must be carried. A low-hit ball might catch that trap, and if such a thing happened, it must definitely end Travers's quest for the open championship. Travers coldly sized up the situation, and then, to the surprise of everyone, picked out his driving iron. I shook my head. He cannot reach the green with that iron, I thought, and he will do mighty well to carry the trap. Jerry knew what he was doing. He took his stance, hit the ball for everything he had in his slight frame, and watched it sail like a bullet toward the trap. There was much doubt as to whether or not it had power sufficient to clear the hazard. The ball was so solidly struck, it made the carry by a margin of three or four yards and bounded forward eight or ten more. It was one of the biggest gambles I have ever seen, that ended successfully. Travers was still forty yards short of the green, but a fine pitch and run, played with a jugger, gave him a four-foot putt for his four, one under par, and he was set now to win. Never wavering on those last three holes, he came in a winner by one stroke over Tom McNamara.

If Travers's victory did nothing else, it established the fact that a great match player could also be a fine medal performer. Just why it was he did not do better in medal competition is one of those unexplainable things, although to my way of thinking it was due to the fact that match play held a greater appeal to him than score play.

The amateur championship was to be played at Detroit. I was the defending champion and Jerry the open titleholder, and this event was unusually interesting. A day or two before the tournament started, a team match was arranged between the East and the West. If I remember correctly, there were eight men on each side. This event meant nothing in so far as importance was concerned, but nevertheless there was much rivalry between the members of the two teams.

I was drawn against Chick Evans, and a big crowd followed our match. The course of the Country Club of Detroit is one of those long and most exacting tests, and Chick, starting with a rush, walked away from me. Along about the middle of the match, I settled down, but could not seem to carve into his three-hole lead. Standing on the sixteenth tee, I was three down and three to play. I won the sixteenth and seventeenth. Now one down, I faced the short eighteenth. The green was a huge one as far as area was concerned, but the pin was placed on the left-hand edge, leaving little room for the ball to land and hold, because it was likewise the most narrow portion. In front was a trap, and there was another just back of the hole. Again I must trust to memory, but it seems to me that, in playing for the flag, from a distance of one hundred and sixty-five yards, there was hardly more than twenty-five feet of green to play to. I could not afford to take the safer direction to the right because I was one down. I had to shoot at the hole. I hit a good shot, but it landed close to

81

the cup and with one bound was over into the trap. Evans naturally played to the right and got on the green, though he was a long way from the hole. I blasted out of the trap ten feet away. Chick rolled his long approach putt five feet from the cup. I holed my putt for a three, and he missed, and the match was square. A four on the nineteenth won for me.

Walking back to the clubhouse, my friend Tom McNamara came to me and said, 'You won two dollars for me.'

'How so?' I replied.

'When you were three down and three to play, a friend of mine offered to bet forty to one against you and I took a nickel's worth,' said Tom.

At a big dinner party that night, favorites for the title were selected and one individual made a substantial wager, giving odds of three to one, that either Travers, Evans, or I would win the championship. We all three qualified without trouble, but Evans was knocked out in the first round by Ned Sawyer and Jerry and myself were stopped in round number two. Many interesting things happened in that championship. In the match between Tom Sherman and Bob Gardner, the firstnamed, playing the short seventh, put his ball twelve inches from the cup. Gardner then stepped up and holed out in one.

Tom's brother Sherrill also can look back on

that seventh hole with amusement. In front of the green was a big ditch, thick with mud. Sherrill in his second-round match barely failed to clear the embankment and his ball rolled back to the edge of the mud. In the process of playing out, he splashed the mud over a nice clean shirt and completely ruined his looks. He was covered, but he succeeded in saving the hole and went on to win the match. The weather was hot and muggy, and Sherrill had so much faith in the magical shirt he refused to change it for a clean one. Therefore, to his own discomfort he wore a golf coat over the shirt and worked his way to the semi-final round before succumbing to John Anderson.

In championship golf the slightest thing can change the complexion of the event and one wee putt can make all the difference in the world. When Max Marston stood on the fourteenth tee, three up and five to play, in the semi-final contest against Bob Gardner, it was almost a certainty that Marston would enter the finals. Nothing can ever be taken for granted, however, in a game of golf. Gardner reduced the lead to the point where he was one down and one to play. You have read of my match with Evans, the eighteenth hole, and the location of the cup. It was in precisely the same spot the day of the Gardner-Marston match.

Gardner played a superb shot that left him a ten-foot putt for a two. Marston striving to protect his lead played to the right and got on the green. He then played a divine approach putt that stopped just fifteen inches from the cup. It was up to Gardner to hole his putt if he was to square the match and send it to extra holes. He putted boldly, too boldly, in fact, and his ball scooted four feet over. As he walked toward the hole, he made a gesture as though he intended to knock Max's ball away, a token of surrender. Then he changed his mind, which he had a perfect right to do, walked up to his own ball, and in a most perfunctory manner tapped it into the hole for a three. Max, anxious to get the match over with, carelessly hit his ball and it rolled around the cup and remained out. It was a heartbreaking miss at such a critical point. That missed putt cost Max a place in the finals, for Gardner won the extra hole without trouble. One can never afford to be careless in a golf match.

The final between Gardner and Anderson was won by the former five up and four to play. Bob was hitting enormous tee shots and following them with long irons to the greens. That championship tournament started with a qualifying round on Saturday, another on Monday, and then five consecutive match-play rounds of thirty-six holes each. As though this was not enough, directly following the final between Gardner and Anderson, an eighteen-hole fourball match was arranged, with

Gardner and Evans against Travers and myself. Bob had previously played thirty-one holes and the extra eighteen gave him a day's work of forty-nine. But he was going just as strong as ever and contributed his share to the winning of the exhibition by four and three.

Another amusing thing happened in Detroit. The Sunday between the first two qualifying rounds, Guilford, Marston, and I were prevailed upon to go to the American League ball park and put on a driving exhibition before a baseball crowd. Detroit was playing the New York Yankees. At the end of five innings, the ball game was stopped and we were ushered out to the home plate. As I teed up a ball on the plate, I could hear someone in the third-base stands shout rather raucously, 'Get those tennis boys off the field and let's have the ball game.' However, we all hit golf balls well over the fence without difficulty, the one driven by Guilford landing on the roof of a house many yards beyond the center-field fence.

After returning from Detroit to Boston, I made arrangements to go into a sporting-goods partnership with my friend Jack Sullivan. About that same time the United States Golf Association had put through a ruling that persons engaged in the sporting-goods business could no longer compete in amateur golf events. Therefore, with my partner and another friend Paul Tewkesbury we were barred

85

as amateur golfers. Then came the War and my partner and I went into the service. I played little golf in 1916, and 1917 saw me playing exhibition matches for the Red Cross just before my reporting to Camp Devens.

In all of my fourball matches I had as my partner Jesse Guilford and we played many a game with Mike Brady and Louis Tellier, the professionals, at the same time raising many dollars for the Red Cross. Mike and I had one individual set-to that was extremely interesting. We had two friends in the automobile industry who were anxious to determine which of us was the better player. I have never liked these matches because they do not prove much, and besides there is no great amount of fun in a match game of golf unless it comes in the usual program of a competition where other men are entered.

However, both Mike and I were willing to play if for no other reason than to satisfy our friends. The only interest I had in the match at all was that of adding to the coffers of the Red Cross. Mike was the professional at the Oakley Country Club and we were to play a home and home game of seventy-two holes, thirty-six at each place. The first half was at Oakley, and though I played two rounds of 72 each, I was six down. Mike was invincible. We repaired to Woodland the next day, and at the end of the morning round I was still six down. I lost the first two holes in the afternoon, which placed me in the most awkward position of being eight down with sixteen to play.

I did not want to be swamped, and standing on that third tee I made up my mind I would give nothing away. In other words, I would play each hole — in fact, each shot — as well as possible. I won the third and fourth. We halved the next two. Mike slipped up on the seventh, and I won that hole. Playing the ninth or sixty-third hole of our match, I stood five down. This was a long two-shotter and I placed my second well on the green. Brady with his second was on the edge of the putting surface. He putted and fell four feet short. I ran my putt close to the hole, and when Mike missed his four-footer, his lead was reduced to four holes.

From the third to the ninth I had not played what could be called a poor shot. After halving the tenth, I won the next two. Now, two down and six to play, I was in a much better position. The thirteenth and fourteenth were halved. The fifteenth was a long hole, par five, and I reached the green in three. I was anxious to win this hole because two of the last three were short holes, and there was little hope of winning those unless I could get down in one putt. Mike was well short of the green with his third and chipped on about ten feet from the cup. To all outward appearances a five seemed likely to win the hole for me, and I coasted my approach putt two feet away. Mike putted, just barely missed, and when his ball stopped on the very edge of the cup, it laid me a dead stymie. There was not a chance to get around his ball, and the only way to win the hole was to pitch in. After much thought the risk seemed too great, because if I touched his ball I was bound to knock it in, and then in place of winning I would lose it and become three down. It was no time to risk such a thing, and I played safely and the hole was halved in six.

After becoming eight up, Brady had deliberately let down, and he was striving to come back, but could not do so. He missed the green on the sixteenth, and I was now but one hole behind him. The match was squared on the long seventeenth where I got a four. We were now playing a hole that measured a hundred and thirty-five yards and I was very keen to win it, and Mike was just as keen to keep me from doing so. I pitched safely on, but left myself a mean downhill putt of ten feet. Brady was short of the hole with an uphill putt. He putted dead, and I now had the ten-footer actually to win the match. I gave little thought to the possibility of rolling well past the cup, because I felt I could drop my ball into the hole for the much-desired two. I hit the thing too boldly and it rolled and rolled, never stopping until it was six feet below. A hasty glance and a quick effort was successful and the match ended all even.

We decided to play it off the following week at Belmont. Mike was not playing well, and I managed to beat him by five up and four to play simply because I took advantage of his errors.

That same year, 1917, the Western Golf Association invited me to compete in their amateur championship, and, though I had not been reinstated by the United States Golf Association as an amateur, on account of my sporting-goods activities, I accepted the invitation and won the Western amateur title. Bobby Jones was one of the contestants, but he was beaten in an early round, which was understandable when one remembers that at the time he was but fifteen years of age.

On the way back from Chicago, I stopped in Rochester to play in a Red Cross match against Walter Hagen. It was a fourball affair, and the scene was Hagen's own course, the Rochester Country Club. My partner and I were three up and five to play. I played those last five holes in one under par, but my partner and I lost four of them and the match. Hagen played those same five holes in 4–3–3–2–3, five better than par.

That fall I was in the United States Army, stationed at Camp Devens, where I had little opportunity to golf, and I remained in the service until January, 1919. In the mean time I had been reinstated by the United States Golf Association, and I looked forward to competing in the amateur championship at Oakmont that summer. I shall never forget that qualifying round at Oakmont as long as I live. An attack of pneumonia in the winter had left me in rather poor condition, but I was quite eager to get back into competition because I had not appeared in any event of importance since the summer of 1915.

With my good friends, Tom Logan and his wife, and my own wife, we motored from Boston to Pittsburgh and on the way out I caught cold. In my weakened condition I developed a fever, which I kept to myself, very foolishly. The day of the first qualifying round was beautiful, and I managed to make a respectable score of 78 on a course that was the most difficult I had ever seen. The 78 was one of the best rounds of the day. The next afternoon I had to play another medal round. Along about the seventh hole the heavens opened and it began to pour with rain. Then it grew very cold and windy and the rain turned to hail. Sevens, eights, and nines began to put in their appearance on my score card as the storm raged. Benches blew over, branches broke from trees, as the velocity of the wind increased every minute. I reached the eighteenth green with my third shot and had two putts for an 86. Only those fellows who played through that storm can imagine the things we faced. The hailstones were pounding away and seemed to be as large as golf balls. It was impossible to putt because the green was covered with the icy missiles. Therefore, I chipped from the green with a midiron and gave myself a putt of not more than ten inches for the 86. Again with the midiron I chipped my ball and, just as it seemed as though nothing could keep it from going in, a huge hailstone dropped directly in front of the ball and kept it out. I got an 87, and was certain that my interest in the championship was ended then and there. The cold and dampness did no good at all to my fever, and I had to go to the clubhouse where a kind-hearted member gave up his room to me.

The storm was directly responsible for the high qualifying scores in this championship. Jimmy Manion, Dave Herron, and Paul Tewkesbury led the field with thirty-six hole totals of 158. Scores as high as 172 qualified, easily the highest ever in the national amateur championship. Oakmont was a severe test, one too difficult when the fury of the elements was taken into consideration.

For several years Chick Evans and I had eluded one another in the match-play rounds simply because we had not been drawn close enough together. At Oakmont in 1919 we had our first official match and it took place in the second round. A bright sun greeted us for a change, and I ap-

peared on the first tee with my fever, and Chick
was suffering from rheumatism. It was a battle of
cripples, and what a battle it turned out to be! As
a golfing classic it lived up to the name in every
sense. On the very first hole, which was a par five,
Evans dropped a forty-five-foot for an eagle three,
and the fun started. There was never more than
a hole difference between us on the first eighteen
holes, and the golf was very fine. As we left for
luncheon, we stood square and neither of us could
eat food of any kind.

I cannot remember the exact details on each
hole of that afternoon round, but I do recall making
five threes on the first eight holes, on three of which
par was four. Standing on the ninth tee, I was two
up and had a four for a 32 for the nine. After
a fine tee shot, I hit a brassie that seemed to split
the pin all the way, but, landing short of the green,
it kicked to the right and ended in a trap. It took
me two to get the ball out of the trap, and Chick
won the hole with a four, leaving me one up with
nine to go. I had played nine holes in 34, three
below par and yet could gain but one.

We had played that stretch of nine holes as brilliantly as possible, and it was out of the question to
continue such golf with physical systems that were
tottering. In no time Chick had evened the match.
Spotty golf developed, but we kept plugging away,
first one and then the other taking the lead.

Finally, standing on the seventeenth tee all square, we drove safely up the hill and short of this well-trapped two hundred and eighty-five yards hole. I had to play my second shot first. With a mashie niblick I pitched over the deep trap six feet from the hole. Chick countered with an even better pitch that stopped three feet away. It was a critical situation. Oftentimes in such a match the fellow who putts first and sinks his putt wins the hole. If he misses, the other chap is almost bound to succeed. Well, in this case we both holed our putts for threes, and staggered to the last tee with the match hinging on one solitary hole. After spending the day battling, we were just where we had started. The eighteenth hole at Oakmont is a grand finishing hole and there is no latitude whatsoever for an errant shot. There was little to choose in the tee shots, for both balls were well down the fairway and within range of the green. My ball was out in front. Chick used a cleek and pulled his ball slightly. It landed short of the green and turned to the left, eventually pulling up in short rough grass just off the putting surface. Now, if I could only place my ball on the green, I should stand a great chance of winning. People lined both sides of the fairway from my ball to the green, and after some thought I selected a mid-iron and played the stroke. It left the club-head satisfactorily, but on the way it developed a wee

93

drift, the result of being shoved, and landed in the sand trap on the right. Fortunately, the ball rolled through the sand and came to rest in the long grass on the bank. On the surface it appeared as though Evans had much the better location, but owing to the fact that I had a fine lie there was no choice. Chick had to play. He chipped too firmly out of the rough and his ball scampered fifteen feet beyond the cup. My ball could not have been more than twenty feet from the flag, even though in the trap, and, as I have said, I had a beautiful lie. As I looked my shot over, I felt reasonably certain that I could pitch it on somewhere near the hole, and it was likewise certain, or almost so, that a four would win that match. A delicate tap sent the ball toward the cup and left me four feet from the goal. Evans putted and missed, and I had only to sink that four-footer to end the festivities. With no thought on anything but the hole, I stroked my ball accurately and it floated as nicely as you please into the cup for the win I wanted so badly.

The next day I had to play Wood Platt, and the winner was to reach the semi-final round. I had never seen Wood Platt hit a ball until that day, and it did not take me long to realize that he was a fine golfer. He had one of the soundest games imaginable with a free and perfect golfing style. Our match was at thirty-six holes and Wood held the upper hand all the way.

Finally, three down and five to go, I managed to square the match, and with lowering skies we set forth for an extra-hole match. I had a long straight tee shot and Wood was yards behind. He was far short of the green with his second. The hole measured four hundred and eighty yards, but the last hundred and eighty was downhill, so that it was within easy reach for me after my drive, and I played a light iron to the middle of the green. Then, as we walked forward, the heavens opened and a perfect deluge of rain poured down upon us. Platt was fifty yards short of the green with a downhill lie. In front of the green was an undulation, and under normal conditions the shot for Platt to play was a pitch and run, because the undulation led to an embankment that formed a sort of plateau, and from there the green sloped away to the back. In other words, a pitch to the green under normal play was out of the question because it was well-nigh impossible to stop such a shot.

The torrent, however, had soaked the fairway, and the undulation in particular was very soggy, so Platt knew he could not play a pitch and run. He had to pitch to a small spot on the bank and trust that the ball would hop forward. That is just what he did. He picked the spot, pitched to it, and the ball rolled gently toward the cup, stopping just an inch away. It was one of the greatest shots under pressure I have ever seen and it earned a half for him. With the rain beating in our faces, we went on to the second extra hole. Wood followed a fine tee shot with a splendid pitch, and the four he got was sufficient to end my championship hopes.

In the mean time Bobby Jones was quietly winning his matches. He got to the finals by beating, in turn, James Manion, Gardner, Rudolph Knepper, and Fownes. In the other half David Herron was bowling his opponents over with great consistency. In the semi-final he took on Wood Platt and beat him by seven up and six to play, which brought about a final between Herron and Jones. Bobby was seventeen years of age, and this was his second amateur championship. Dave was playing his home course and knew every roll on the greens, and he putted brilliantly all day long. A tremendous gallery followed the players as Dave whipped himself into a lead by fine golf and finer putting. Herron leading by four up, they came to the long twelfth and Bobby hit a very long tee shot straight down the middle. Just as he was at the top of his swing and prepared to hit a brassie shot, one of the marshals, with a megaphone in hand, saw fit to speak to the gallery. In a loud tone of voice he shouted, and Jones, completely unsettled, topped his ball into a trap a few yards in front, and he never recovered thereafter, eventually losing by five and four.

It was in this championship that I had an unusual experience in my first-round match with
Eddie Cleary. Playing the sixteenth, a one-shot
hole, I put my ball on the front edge of the green.
At the time I was one up and three to play. Cleary
sliced badly to boggy ground on the right, and after
searching for a minute or two, I discovered a ball
embedded in the mud. Cleary naturally thought it
was his ball, and proceeded to knock it out of the
muck. He put his third on the green and his ball
was completely covered with mud. He was a long
way from the hole. The green was very fast and
my putt was downhill. I figured Cleary could do
no better than a five, so I putted firmly and my ball
rolled ten or twelve feet below the cup. You see,
I wanted to leave myself an uphill putt. Had I
putted cautiously, I could well have stopped my
ball above the hole and then perhaps have slipped
by so far that I should end up by taking four putts
and let Cleary off the hook. I was taking no such
chance. Eddie put his approach putt stone dead,
which gave me two for the hole. And I took the
two putts. Cleaning the mud from the ball he had
played, Cleary discovered it was not his at all. The
rule is clear and says that, where the player plays
more than two shots with the wrong ball, he loses
the hole.

Our referee was Howard Whitney, President of
the United States Golf Association. Since it was

97

I who had found the ball that we thought belonged to Cleary, I appealed to the referee for a replay. It could not be done and halving the next hole, the match ended. I felt sorry for Cleary, because he might have earned a half had he played the proper ball, but Howard Whitney explained that his play undoubtedly affected my play and consequently the rule could not be waived.

Francis, seven, with his parents in front of their home at 246 Clyde
Street, Brookline, Mass. Courtesy of the Ouimet Foundation

Ouimet with Harry Varden and Ted Ray outside the clubhouse at The
Country Club, 1913 Open. Courtesy of the Ouimet Foundation

"Francis in Action." Courtesy of the Ouimet Foundation

Ouimet hits from the sand, U.S. Open, 1913.
Courtesy of United States Golf Association

Ouimet follows through, 1913.
Courtesy of United States Golf Association

"Francis in Full Form, 1913." Courtesy of the Ouimet Foundation

Ouimet teeing-off on the thirteenth hole at The Country Club,
USGA Open playoff, 1913. Courtesy of the Ouimet Foundation

Ouimet lines up his putt on the eighteenth hole at
The Country Club in the playoff vs. Vardon and Ray.
Courtesy of the Ouimet Foundation

Ouimet wins the 1914 U.S. Amateur, Ekwanok Country Club,
Manchester, Vermont. Courtesy of United States Golf Association

Francis Ouimet and Bobby Jones (R.T. Jones), 1920.
Courtesy of United States Golf Association

Ouimet with British great Roger H. Wethered, 1923 British Amateur, Deal, England. Courtesy of United States Golf Association

Ouimet wins his second National Amateur, Beverly Hills, Illinois, 1931. Courtesy of United States Golf Association

On the eighth Fairway at Beverly Hills.
Courtesy of the Ouimet Foundation

Ouimet with golf legend Walter Hagen.
Courtesy of United States Golf Association

Ouimet poses near the tee.
Courtesy of United States Golf Association

Ouimet greets British star Jack Westland.
Courtesy of the Ouimet Foundation

Eddie Lowery and Francis Ouimet are reunited at the U.S. Open,
The Country Club, 1963. Courtesy of the Ouimet Foundation

Ouimet "drives in" as he is inducted as the first American elected
captain of the Royal and Ancient Golf Club of St. Andrews, 1951.
Courtesy of the Ouimet Foundation

Ouimet wears the famous "Red Jacket" as the captain of the Royal
and Ancient, 1951. Courtesy of the Ouimet Foundation

Ouimet with President Dwight D. Eisenhower, avid golfer and
portrait painter of Ouimet in his St. Andrew's "Red Jacket."
Courtesy of United States Golf Association

Ouimet as honorary chairman gives trophy to Julius Boros,
U.S. Open Champion, 1963, The Country Club.
Courtesy of the Ouimet Foundation

The Francis Ouimet
Commemorative Stamp,
1963. Courtesy of the
Ouimet Foundation

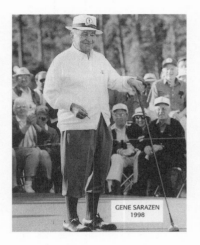

Golf legend Gene Sarazen, a great
friend to Ouimet. Courtesy of the
Ouimet Foundation

Ben Crenshaw, surrounded by the Ryder Cup caddies, receives his
copy of the "Francis and Eddie" portrayal with sculptor Robert Pack.
Courtesy of the Ouimet Foundation

CHAPTER VI

PLAYING WITH OUR COUSINS THE BRITONS

FROM time to time British golfers appeared in our championships, but 1920 was the first time that a strong group came from the other side. That year, Lord Charles Hope, Tommy Armour, Cyril Tolley, and one or two more entered the championship that was played at the Engineers' Club, Roslyn, Long Island. There was such a large list of entries, it was decided to double up on two courses for the qualifying round, eighteen to be played at Engineers' and eighteen at the neighboring North Shore Country Club. Engineers' was a difficult layout, and owing to this, there was much congestion. The result was that those who played at Engineers' in the morning were delayed tremendously in their later round because of the amount of time consumed in rushing from one course to the other.

Armour was the only one of the Britons to qualify. Fred Wright and Bobby Jones tied for the low score, and the highest total to survive was 165. The champion Herron had a hard match in the first round. He was playing a youth named Peter Harmon, and at the end of thirty-six holes the pair were even. They carried on in the dark to the thirty-ninth, and here Harmon hooked three balls apparently out of bounds and gave up the hole. I understand that the following morning the first two were found in bounds, but from their position in the rough, it is unlikely the outcome of the match would have been changed.

In the second round, Chick Evans had a battle with Reggie Lewis, entered from Greenwich, Connecticut, that he will never forget. Lewis was capable of playing brilliant golf, and he was very much on his game the day he played Chick. Playing the thirty-sixth hole and standing one up, Lewis drove a beautiful long tee shot straight down the middle of the fairway. The last hole at Engineers' was a testing two-shotter, and the green was in poor condition. The drainage or something was not right and the result was that hardly a spear of grass could be grown. Evans needed that hole badly. He needed length, too, and, striving to get a bit more distance, he pulled his ball to a trap on the left. He could not possibly get home on his second. However, his ball was lying well and he wanted to get as near the green as possible, so he chose a wooden club with which to play out of the trap. This he pulled and the ball sailed away to the left toward some trees. It crashed into a stout oak and rebounded to the fairway just a few yards in front of where Lewis's tee shot had stopped. The beauty of the game of golf lies in its uncertainties.

Lewis, eager to win, smashed a long iron to the back of the green which had all the appearances of the clinching shot. He was sure to get a five, perhaps a four, and the best that Evans seemed likely to do was a five. Therefore, everything pointed to a Lewis victory. Chick hit a great shot to the green and about twenty feet from the hole. Even that did not change the complexion of the match any, because Reggie chipped six feet away on the like.

Evans always has been a marvelous golfer, and yet one of the most unsuccessful putters I have ever seen. If Jerome Travers had been in Chick's position, I should say Jerry would at least hit the hole on his effort, but not Chick. And again the green was so uneven, it merely added to his difficulties. Well, Chick stepped up and stroked his ball as smoothly as could be into the hole for a four. You can talk about your critical putts, but here was one. Lewis now had to sink his six-footer. He barely missed, and the two moved on to extra holes. First one and then the other missed holeable putts to win on the first four extra holes. Finally, Evans dropped a putt of four feet on the fifth, the forty-first hole of their match, to win.

I bumped into Tommy Armour in the third round. Tommy was very wild starting away, and I won the first five holes, and it was just as well I did. Finishing the eighteen five up, I was in a seemingly secure spot. In the afternoon I was treated to one of the most bizarre golfing exhibitions that it has been my privilege to witness. My own score for nine holes was thirty-seven, and there was hardly a blemish in my play, yet Tommy was thirty-four to the turn and had won back three holes. Fortunately for me, he let up a bit and I recovered the lost holes to win, five and four. Those five holes in the morning did the trick, which proves that it is well to win every hole that you can.

After his first-round scare, Evans bowled everybody aside, and got to the finals. As a general rule in an amateur championship, the finalists on the road have at least one match that gives them plenty of bother, and in Chick's case it was the Lewis affair that caused him his greatest anxiety. After turning aside Armour, my semi-final opponent was none other than the boy wonder from Atlanta, Bobby Jones. He was eighteen years of age, had performed wonderfully well in amateur competition, and that summer had entered his first open championship, played at Inverness. Ted Ray won this tournament, but Bobby showed he was not a flash in the pan by finishing only four strokes behind the winner.

I had the greatest respect in the world for Bobby's play and fully prepared myself for the stiffest sort of a contest. As I think of Jones now and his game in 1920, I see but one difference. In 1920 he was just as great, with the exception of his work on the greens, and I must say he was not even a fair putter then. I beat him six up and five to play, simply because I putted better than he. On green after green he required three putts, and these mistakes either permitted me to win holes or halve some where I had erred on the way. As an instance of what Bobby did on the greens, let us take the eighteenth hole in the morning. My second shot was wide of the green and Bobby was plumb on. At the time I was three up. I chipped on eight feet from the hole and missed the putt for a four. Bobby ran a fine long approach putt two feet from the cup and then, to the surprise of all, he missed, letting me get away with a half. In the afternoon I lost the first hole by being trapped with my second, but after a series of halves I won the seventh, eighth, and ninth holes, to increase my lead to five at the twenty-seventh. The end came on the fourteenth, where with a par four I finished the match.

East *versus* West and another match between Evans and myself was on for the amateur championship of the United States. One of the features of this championship, apart from the golf itself, was the fact that stymies had been abolished. For years there had been much agitation stirred up against the stymie, and, after giving the matter considerable thought, the United States Golf Association decided to give any player who was stymied by an opponent the option of playing the stymie or conceding the opponent a putt, and having a clear road between his ball and the hole. It is not for me to say whether or not the rule was a good one, because it had little bearing on the matches I had played in. As I think of it, I believe there was too much picking up of balls on the greens and some of the concessions of eight- and ten-foot putts were ludicrous.

Chick and I started our play on a warm September Saturday, and we were extremely cautious, each feeling the other out, as it were. The first four holes were halved, and the first real opportunity for me to take the lead happened on the fifth. Evans was short of the green on his second, short again with his third, and about four feet away with his fourth. My second was over, and I chipped down toward the hole, the ball stopping five feet from the cup. Taking into consideration the roll of the green, Evans's ball was dangerously close to the line I had to take. I gave the matter much thought. I could concede Chick his putt for a five and have a free, unimpeded putt to win the hole. At the very worst, I could get a half.

Then I was struck by a psychological thought which I decided to put into effect. That was to try and slide by Evans's ball. If I succeeded, the hole was mine. If I failed, Chick must then sink his tricky four-footer to save the hole for himself.

If he missed, it might have an effect upon his confidence. Therefore, I elected to gamble. I putted and missed. Chick putted and succeeded, and the hole was halved. At the turn we were square. Then Chick turned loose in earnest and rattled off a brilliant thirty-four to end the morning round three holes to the good. His play was magnificent and his putting left nothing to be desired. He had hit his stride, and continued to split the fairways with his tee shots, following these with super-irons. I just could not stay near him. At the twenty-seventh hole I was seven holes down. Beginning with the tenth in the morning and through the ninth in the afternoon, a total of eighteen consecutive holes, Evans had taken exactly 69 strokes on one of the longest, toughest, and trickiest courses I have ever played. The tenth was one hundred and eighty-five yards in length. Chick played a fine iron eight feet from the cup. I was struggling and had my back set against the wall, but where there is life there is hope, and I planted a jigger shot stone dead. On this same hole in the qualifying round, Cyril Tolley took a nine, so this will give you some idea of those two shots, because they were exceptional. Evans had not looked like missing a putt, and he stepped forward gingerly but confidently and stroked his ball into the hole for a two. The record for Engineers' was 71, and yet Chick was 71 for nineteen straight holes. The end came on the twelfth green, where Chick won seven up and six to play. I had no regrets at all, because I was simply outclassed by a great player. The usually weak armament in his game, putting, stood out like a beacon, and I decided then and there Chick was the finest putter I had ever played against.

With the exception of 1919, when Davidson Herron won and Jones was runner-up, it was difficult for the younger generation to break through the seasoned campaigners. The championship of 1920 brought forth a new crop of young stars, and though they did not win, they were beginning to establish themselves in no uncertain manner. During the winter of 1920–21, it was decided to send a team of American amateurs to England for the purpose of playing a team of British amateurs in an informal match. G. Herbert Walker had donated the cup, known as the Walker Cup, a year before, and it was hoped an international contest could be arranged, hence the informal beginning.

The team selected by the United States Golf Association consisted of Charles Evans, Robert T. Jones, Jr., Jesse Guilford, Paul Hunter, J. Wood Platt, W. C. Fownes, Fred Wright, and myself. On the British side were Tolley, Jenkins, Montmorency, Simpson, Aylmer, Armour, Holderness, and Wethered. Surely on form shown they were strong and evenly matched teams. The British amateur championship was to be played at Hoylake, a course outside of Liverpool, and it was decided to have the team match played there also.

Unfortunately, Great Britain had had but little rain for six or seven months and the Hoylake fairways and greens were like concrete, quite different from American fairways and watered putting greens. In the practice sessions, we invariably played one round well and the next would be very poor. As an example of what I am getting at, Bobby Jones played a brilliant 71 one morning, and that same afternoon his score was well above 80. It seemed impossible to get two good scores consecutively. Most of the Americans had little knowledge of how to play a running shot, the only safe one with which to approach the greens. Their high pitches would light on the greens and bound merrily over.

After a week of trials and tribulations, the day for the team match arrived. The contest consisted of eighteen holes of foursome play and then eighteen holes of singles competition. We felt we could hold our own in the singles matches, but there were many misgivings about foursome play. Guilford and I had had some experience in this form of play, which is a feature of Lesley Cup competition. The same could be said of Fownes, but to the other Americans it was a new game. The British players indulge frequently in foursomes, and therefore it was expected that they would win most of these matches.

To the surprise of everyone, the Americans swept the foursome matches completely, every pair winning, which sent us away with a four-point lead. Of the eight singles matches, five were won by our boys, and with it the team match by nine points to three. It was a great start, but in spite of this, we felt none too confident over our chances in the individual championship owing to the treachery of the course.

There was one hole in particular that bothered the players, and did more toward breaking the confidence of the American golfers than any other. The fourth was a hole of about one hundred and thirty-five yards, with a trap in front of the green. It was simple enough to pitch over the trap, but the trick was to hold the ball on the green. Time and again a finely hit mashie would send the ball high in the air, but once it hit the green, it went bounding far beyond. One evening we were discussing the proper way to play to the green of this hole, but no one seemed able to advance a convincing method. Jesse Guilford, who is never very talkative, spoke up and said, 'There is only one way to play that hole successfully, and that is to miss your mashie shot.' We all laughed heartily. Jesse went on to say that he played the hole twice that day, missed his mashie shot badly each time, and the ball, landing short of the trap, bounded over it to the green and stopped close enough so that he experienced little difficulty in getting a pair of twos. That was certainly a brand-new angle, but one that required altogether too much finesse for any of the boys to try.

Our strength was considerably reduced owing to an accident to Wood Platt which kept him out of the championship. He tripped and fell and landed on the corner of a steamer trunk which cut his knee cap so badly that he could not play. Everyone else was in fine playing form, with the exception of Fred Wright, and his game was terribly erratic. No one gave Fred much thought as a championship possibility and the favorites among our forces were Jones, Evans, and Guilford.

One by one the Americans disappeared from the event, Evans losing to Fownes, who in turn was beaten by Wright. Guilford was beaten by Tolley in a great match. Playing the twelfth hole, Guilford hit a prodigious tee shot down the fairway and his ball ended in a rabbit hole, which proved fatal. That match was even at the time, so the incident did not please Jesse a bit. Jones was put out by Allan Graham six up and five to play in a match in which Jones could not sink a putt over two feet. The weak member, Fred Wright, continued to improve all along the line, and when the last eight survivors were made known, Wright was the soli-

109

tary American left. Wright was to play against my friend, the well-known British writer, Bernard Darwin, and they had a great match. Even at the end of eighteen holes, they continued to the nineteenth, where Darwin won.

The British amateur championship was won easily by a youthful English lad named Willie Hunter, since turned professional. If ever a golfer adapted himself to conditions, it was Willie Hunter. He was the only player in the field who played the pitch-and-run shot successfully, and he got better and better in his art as he progressed toward the title.

Jones and Paul Hunter remained over to compete in the British open at St. Andrews. Bobby started well enough in the open, but in the third round he got tangled up in a trap on the short eleventh hole, and he tore up his card. It is the only time in his brilliant golfing record that Bobby has seen fit to do such a thing. I believe he was just a little homesick and wanted a good reason for leaving St. Andrews in time to catch a steamer back home.

On our way to St. Andrews, driving with our friends Mr. and Mrs. Thomas Logan, we stopped off at Turnberry for the purpose of seeing the ladies' championship. Alexa Stirling was the foremost American lady golfer entered and she was drawn against Cecil Leitch in the first or second round. It was hailed as one of the greatest matches ever played between women, because Miss Stirling was easily the best golfer of her sex in this country and Miss Leitch was the outstanding British player.

Turnberry is one of those typical seaside courses, situated near the Irish Sea and not far from Robert Bruce's castle. Looking out to sea is a huge rock called Ailsa Craig, completely surrounded by water, and it made a tremendous impression upon me as it stood like a huge fortress in the middle of the emerald-colored water. To add further to the color of the match, the day itself was overcast and windy, a testing one for the two great golfers. Miss Leitch proved better equipped in power to withstand the rigors of that cold and windy day and beat her American rival after much fine golf had been played. In that championship was a girl, Joyce Wethered, who was fast developing into a great golfer.

At the conclusion of the Stirling-Leitch contest, I dropped back with a few people to follow Miss Wethered. She was having a close match with a player whose name does not come to me at the moment. Miss Wethered's play in that high wind impressed me most favorably, for she seemed to have superb control over her ball at all times. Playing to the seventeenth, she led by one hole. That particular hole was really difficult, since it was a three-shotter for the women, and a nasty wind swept across the line of play from right to left. Such a wind is in my opinion the most difficult of all winds to play against, because the common tendency is to play the ball to the right and allow for wind driftage.

Miss Wethered had hit a fine drive and brassie down the fairway and was left with an iron shot of perhaps a hundred and twenty yards to the green. I have seen any number of first-class male golfers under similar conditions play well to the right, allowing the wind to bring the ball back on line. I observed Miss Wethered closely to see just what she would do. Out came a straight-faced iron club from her bag and she took her stance. A short back swing and a smart, decisive stroke met the ball. It traveled low and started to the left, and then began to turn into the wind. The ball was hit hard enough to accentuate the curve as it bored ahead. The wind tried hard to blow that ball off line, but it was too skillfully struck to permit of such a thing. Finally landing on the green, it took one hop and stopped dead in its tracks three feet from the cup. That was enough for me, because then and there I decided I had seen the finest woman golfer of them all. Miss Wethered reached the final round, to be beaten by Miss Leitch, but she had definitely established herself as a great golfer which later years have conclusively proved. As with Bobby Jones, some day someone may come along to take her place in the sun, but so long as golf is played, it will be difficult to visualize one better than Joyce Wethered.

CHAPTER VII

'THE GREATEST LITTLE SHOTS'

The American amateur championship was played at St. Louis. Willie Hunter and Tommy Armour came over from the other side to compete. Chandler Egan brought a group of fine youngsters from the Pacific Northwest; Von Elm was there, and practically every good golfer in the country. It was my good fortune to win the qualifying medal with rounds of 69 and 75. From there the scores ran to 162, the top figure to get in. Both Hunter and Armour were real championship threats, Hunter scoring 154 and Tommy 155 for the two rounds.

The champion, Chick Evans, also qualified with ease, but he had a most harrowing experience on the short twelfth hole. This hole measured about one hundred and eighty yards in length and the green was situated in a semi-punchbowl on a high piece of ground. Always a splendid iron player, Chick hit a beautiful shot to the green, not more than fifteen feet from the hole. He had a chance to tie for the medal up to that point, and his game was as sound as a rock. His first putt very nearly dropped for a two, but it slipped by on the fast green four feet. He putted again rather quickly and missed. This upset him no little. Then, with

114

one hand he tried to tap a wee putt into the hole, missed, and while the ball was moving, he hit it again and once more it failed to sink. There was a penalty for hitting a ball in motion, and when the smoke cleared away, Chick had to put a seven on the card. Six putts from fifteen feet comes near to being a record! From there in, Evans just poked along, content to qualify.

In the first round I had to play my old rival Max Marston. At the finish of the first round, I was four down. While awaiting luncheon, I sat on the porch and went over the morning round and could not quite understand how it was that I was so many holes down to Max. I knew he played well, but in my thoughts I did not believe there was a difference of four holes in the quality of our play. While still in deep thought, I dropped off into a sound sleep and after a few moments I awoke with a start. I had been dreaming of our match, and in the dream I decided most of the four holes I had lost had slipped away because of inattentiveness. A missed shot here and there for no good reason accounted for the discrepancy.

Away we went in the afternoon, and Max won the first hole to increase his lead to five. I pulled myself together and played the next eleven holes in 36, three over threes, and not only wiped out the five holes, but got myself a two-hole lead in the bargain. On that stretch I had scored twos on each of the short holes, and had two threes besides. It was just as well for me that the streak came when it did, because Max never let up for a minute, and I was pleased when the match ended in my favor on the thirty-fifth green by two and one.

Harrison Johnston finished me the next day in a match that went the full route of thirty-six holes. Just at a time when I needed my best putting stroke, it left me completely, and toward the end I could not putt the ball into a six-foot barrel. The course was playing very slow, owing to evening rains and irrigated fairways, a distinct contrast to conditions we had faced at Hoylake, where Willie Hunter won the British amateur title. Hunter proved his ability to meet any conditions successfully by beating Bobby Jones in the third round. It was generally thought that, because Hunter was not a long hitter, he would find plenty of trouble getting home in two on the par four holes. He had no difficulty at all, and his putting and approaching were superb all day long.

Evans in the mean time had gained the semifinal bracket in the upper half with Jesse Guilford and Hunter in the lower had to play Bob Gardner. The morning of those matches it rained like fury, and Guilford, long noted for his ability to plough around golf courses in the rain and mud, beat the champion by five and four. Gardner, too, had little difficulty in dismissing the remaining British entry.

Gardner had won the championship in 1909 and 1915, and had been runner up in 1916, so his position in the finals was not new to him. On the other hand, it was Guilford's first experience and he made the most of it. He was driving a tremendous tee shot and very straight, and his putting and iron play were as near perfection as anything could be. Four up in the morning, he kept adding a hole here and there until the match came to an end in his favor by eight up and seven to play. Jesse is not a great talker, or rather he hates to make speeches. He was presented the championship cup and the gold medal, before the St. Louis spectators, and called upon to say a word or two. He blushed from head to foot, and quietly said, 'If I am expected to give a speech, I am sorry I won the title.'

The standard of American amateur golf was rising steadily, and no longer was it an event for two or three players. There were any number of splendid young players fully able to hold their own in any company, and of course the outstanding one among them was Bobby Jones. Von Elm and Sweetser were coming fast, to say nothing of ten or a dozen more. In 1922, the Walker Cup matches were instituted, an outcome of the informal game at Hoylake. Great Britain sent an eight-man team to this country to play in that competition, which was won by the American side, eight matches to four. The result really did not represent the true

117

picture, for with an exception here and there all matches were extremely close. The contest was played at Southampton, over the National Golf Links of America, truly one of the fine courses of the world.

From Southampton the players moved along to the Country Club at Brookline for the amateur championship. I shall never forget that second qualifying round — first, on account of the weather, and next, because of a round of golf that must go down as one of the greatest that has ever been played by anybody. It started to rain the morning of that second round, and it rained so hard that in no time the polo field, which served as a fairway to both the first and eighteenth holes, looked more like a lake, with dozens of islands here and there, than a well-kept fairway. Tees got so muddy it was almost impossible to stand up and hit a tee shot. Greens were covered with casual water, and still it rained. Bobby Jones had scored a 73 in the pouring rain, and his thirty-six-hole total stood uncontested at 145 for a long time.

The champion, Jesse Guilford, was out in the worst of the storm. Ready-made tees of wood were not in existence at the time, and if they were, I doubt if they would have served the purpose for which they were intended, because they could hardly support the weight of the ball. I finished my round, got cleaned up, and went to the tenth tee to see how Guilford was getting along. Jesse had started away with a sweater that came down to his belt-line, but after playing nine holes, it looked more like an overcoat than a sweater. I offered him an umbrella, which he spurned with the statement that an umbrella could not help him at that stage of the game. He was glad to get a rubber tee, because the sand simply melted under the ball the instant it was placed on the ground. He had reached the turn in 37, a wonderful score. He played that last nine in 33. The divots he raised after each iron shot resembled rabbit-skins, but his ball always landed and stopped at the hole-side. His 70 added to the 74 gave him the medal.

Five British players qualified, three of whom had represented their country in the Walker Cup matches. These were Colin Aylmer, Willie Torrance, and Cyril Tolley. The other two, Tommy Armour and Willie Hunter, had taken up a residence in this country, and therefore were not eligible for their Walker Cup team. Guilford worked his way to the third round and was beaten by Jesse Sweetser. The latter had put out of the way two good men in Hunter and Guilford, and was playing beautifully. Rudolph Knepper dropped me in the second round, so there was nothing to do but watch the other boys.

Four great players came together in the semifinals; Sweetser against Jones and Evans against

Knepper. Ordinarily such matches should have been hard-fought and close, but just the reverse was the case. Evans defeated Knepper by eleven up and ten to play to reach one part of the finals and Sweetser completely subdued Bobby eight up and seven. Sweetser had been getting better with each round, and the morning of his semi-final with Jones he scored a 69 and led by five holes.

A most unusual thing happened on the second hole. It is a par four, calling for a well-placed drive, and the player is then left with an optional shot — that is, either a pitch to the green or a pitch and run. After two fine tee shots, Sweetser took out a club which he used for approach work and played a shot that traveled about fifty yards and rolled into the hole for a two. Bobby had to sink his ball from about the same distance for a half. He played an exquisite shot that landed at the front edge of the green and then rolled like a well-stroked putt right for the hole. It lost its speed three feet away and finally died six inches short of the cup. Bernard Darwin characterized those two shots as, 'The greatest little shots' he had ever seen.

Sweetser won the final from Evans by beating the old master at his own game. His iron play was a thing of beauty, and, pitching his shots with a ribbed-face club, he was constantly inside Chick all day long. The match was close for all that. Playing the thirteenth, Sweetser was two up.

Evans followed a good tee shot with a magnificent iron that left his ball six feet from the pin. It was just the time for him to do something like that, especially if he was going to win, for one hole can be made up sometimes where it is impossible to get the other. Jesse took plenty of time. He sized up the situation as though he realized its full importance. Once his mind was made up, he acted. High in the air and straight at the flag flew his ball. It came down on the green with a thud and a hop and settled stone dead. That was too much for the gallant Evans, and he missed his putt that would have halved that hole. Three up now, Sweetser clung to his lead as a drowning man grasps at a straw and victory finally perched on his shoulder on the sixteenth green.

America was sending a team abroad for the Walker Cup matches in 1923, and I was favored with an invitation. It was to be my third trip to England, and I looked forward with hopes that I should do something worth while. For some reason or other I had been unable to play as well abroad as at home, and I decided it was because of too much golf beforehand. The Americans entered the St. George's Cup contest at Sandwich, an event calling for thirty-six holes of medal play. The British championship was to be played at Deal, which was hard-by Sandwich, and in consequence we were keen to get into condition for the title event.

A Game of Golf

One of our team members, Doctor Willing, led the field the first eighteen holes with a 74, and our Captain Gardner was next, a stroke more. I was grouped with several players at 77. The next day I scored a 76 and Doctor Willing was 79, but our total of 153 was low. In the play-off for the St. George's Gold Vase, we had a hot struggle. On the fourth hole I played a long spoon shot that stopped two feet from the hole, and I picked up two strokes. The battling Doctor kept everlastingly at it, and got within one stroke of me time and again, but I hung on, and finally left the eighteenth tee with a two-stroke lead.

We hit good tee shots down the middle, and the Doctor, playing the second shot first, shoved his ball off to the right and into the rough. The eighteenth green at Sandwich is rather small and terraced and difficult to play to. Seeing the Doctor's predicament, I deliberately kept my ball short of the green, figuring that a five would be enough to carry me safely through and at the same time leave me an opportunity of approaching over safe country. The Doctor had a devilish shot to play. His ball not only lay in long grass, but directly between it and the hole was a sand trap. Just over the trap was the green which sloped away from him. He had to hit his ball firmly enough to clear the trap and then he had to be careful that it did not strike the downhill grade. Doctor Willing is a wonder on or around the putting greens. With a gentle flick of the wrist he lofted the ball barely over the trap and it rolled slowly down the incline toward the hole. It hit the back of the cup, not rolling too hard, and how it ever stayed out is beyond me, but it did stop out. I had three to get down, to win the St. George's Cup, and believe me I tried nothing fancy and took all three.

Then on to Deal for the amateur championship. In connection with a British amateur championship there is a contest that for interest and rivalry beats anything I have ever seen. It is the annual team match between England and Scotland. Foursomes are played in the morning and singles in the afternoon, and the competition is played the Saturday before the championship which starts the following Monday. We had practiced diligently over the Deal course and we discovered it needed plenty of knowing. George Rotan was on our team, as were Sweetser, Wright, Gardner, Johnston, Herron, Marston, Doctor Willing, and Jack Neville.

Fearing that we might wear ourselves out with too much practice, George and I, in lieu of playing, often walked around the course and studied it. The American boys were invited to the dinner of the Scottish and English teams after their match with the understanding that they would not be called upon for a speech. Out of a clear sky Rotan was called to his feet. George is never lost for something to say and promptly responded that the only speech he had prepared was the one he was going to give after the finals. It brought down the house and he started to seat himself, but our British friends would not stand for it.

Rotan stood up again and good-naturedly asked the gathering what they would like to have him say. Someone said, 'Give us your impressions of the Deal course.' George looked toward the person for a second, and then calmly said, 'I think the rough here at Deal is the finest I have ever tried to play out of.' That let him off.

I managed to reach the semi-final round at Deal, but Roger Wethered was altogether too hot for me. My aspirations to win the British amateur title dropped with a resounding bang when Roger outplayed me on the last nine.

That trip of 1923 stands out in my memory as one of the grandest golfing excursions I have ever taken. In the first place, we played informal matches at Rye, against a team of Oxford and Cambridge golfers, and also at Woking with a team made up of fellows who called themselves the Moles. For a long time I could not quite get the connection as to why they called themselves the Moles. One of their members, good old Bob Harris, who has always been charming to American players, told me it was an organization got together to spend a pleasant day in the country. Besides visiting Canterbury and other places of historic interest, we were splendidly entertained by the Pilgrim Society, and also at the House of Commons. At the dinner given to the Americans at the House of Commons we had the pleasure of meeting many of the conspicuous figures in British public life, among them Lloyd George and Sir John Simon.

CHAPTER VIII

ST. ANDREWS AND ROGER WETHERED

ST. ANDREWS is really and truly the golfers' Paradise. Everybody in that town of some six thousand residents is interested in the game. Male and female, children and elderly people, all play golf in some form or other. There is a hotel called 'Golf Hotel,' but for that matter all hotels or boarding-houses harbor golfers. There are golf shops everywhere where one can buy anything from a club or ball to a golf suit or a fancy-colored golf umbrella.

In 1923, the American boys had reservations at the Grand Hotel, which was less than a fair-sized approach putt from the eighteenth green. In late May or early June, the twilight of the long Scottish evenings carries on to eleven o'clock. It was nothing at all unusual to see fourball matches coming up the eighteenth fairway as late as ten-thirty, and since American golfers were in the habit of retiring at that hour, after thirty-six holes of golf, they were often rocked to sleep by the click of club-heads meeting balls.

The wonderful club, known as the Royal and Ancient, should not be forgotten, because it adds to the dignity of the place. This, of course, is where

126

the rules of golf were laid down and every development of the clubs and balls has its own cabinet for displaying the implements that have given to the world at large so much pleasure. Magnificent trophies, too, are sights well worth the golfer's interest. A simple stone building, one can recline in the easy-chairs and think of nothing but the most pleasant things. It is the atmosphere that is so thrilling — golf and nothing but golf.

A few practice rounds and the Walker matches of 1923 were on — both sides eager to win, but placing the mere winning as secondary to the game itself. The first event was the foursome play, and the teams were arranged as follows:

Sweetser-Ouimet   *vs.* Wethered-Tolley
Gardner-Marston   *vs.* Harris-Hooman
Rotan-Herron   *vs.* Holderness-Hope
Johnston-Neville   *vs.* Wilson-Murray

The British team won three of the four matches and stepped into a lead that was considered impregnable. The only American winners were Gardner and Marston. In order to retain the Walker Cup, the Americans had to win five of the eight singles matches, which might really only bring about a tie, since by losing three the Britons would still have the same total of six points. However, in the event of a tie the Cup is retained by the previous winner. For the singles Fred Wright and

Doctor Willing took the places of Harrison Johnston and Jack Neville and away we went.

I was paired against Roger Wethered in number one place. In the morning round there was never a time when every American, with the exception of Bob Gardner, was not several holes down to a British opponent. I remember at luncheon we got together, figured how many holes each of us was down, and, taking our worst deficit at any stage of our matches, we were twenty-seven holes behind our opponents. I bring this up merely to show what an uncertain game golf is. George Rotan found himself six down with four to play against Willis MacKenzie, in the first eighteen holes, each match being thirty-six; he won the last four holes to stand two behind, and then went out in the afternoon and won seven of the first eight, the other being halved. Rotan had won eleven out of twelve successive holes, and what was more, the match by six up and four to play.

My own match with Roger Wethered was a classic. He had beaten me at Deal in the semi-finals of the British amateur event, and I was naturally quite anxious to turn the tables on him if possible. In the morning I could not hold him, and Roger ended that session two holes to the good. After luncheon we got together again, and our match bristled with high-class golf. Just as it appeared as though I might get somewhere, Roger would hole a putt the length of the green to shut me off.

Playing the ninth or twenty-seventh hole of our match, I thought I had a fine chance to win and square the match. His second shot was at least forty feet from the cup, on a green that was as fast as lightning. If he could place his putt dead, it seemed he would be accomplishing a miracle. My second left me a ten-footer. Roger putted his transcontinental putt and holed it. The shock was too much for me, and instead of being square or only one down, I was two down again.

I was out in 35, the same as Roger. On the way in I picked up the thirteenth hole and was one down. The fourteenth hole at St. Andrews is four hundred and fifty-six yards long, par five, but reachable in two with a favoring wind. We had that. On the way is the famous Hell bunker, a veritable graveyard to anybody who fetches it. The wind eliminated this possibility, because it was easy to carry that day. I put a second on the green, which is no small trick owing to countless contours that normally toss your ball in any but the proper direction. Wethered followed suit with a fine iron that rolled for the pin, but the ball was hit too well, and it rolled over the back edge.

It seemed at last as if I could square the match, because Roger from the other side of the green had an almost impossible approach to make. Then he handed me the cruelest blow of all. He used his putter, rolled the ball up the embankment to the green, and then calmly watched it wend its way without interference into the cup for a three. It was one of the most devastating putts I have ever seen. My perfectly good four, one under par, was just as useless as a ten. We had an enormous gallery, made interesting by the red capes worn by the students of St. Andrews University, who take every opportunity to follow a golf match.

The holes were fast running out, and I was two down and four to go. We halved the fifteenth, which only postponed the agony. The sixteenth that day was a drive and a short approach, the hole measuring about three hundred and sixty yards or so. The short way to the hole is naturally straight at it, but the attendant risks are traps on the left and the railroad tracks on the right. But the tracks are no place to drive, anyway, because they are out of bounds, and the penalty for such a shot is stroke and distance. There was no occasion for Roger to drive toward the green, because he was nursing a two-hole advantage. Therefore, he hammered a long ball well to the left and perfectly safe. With me it was different. I had to gamble. There was no chance at all to drive the green, but I wanted to get as near it as possible. I drove my ball down along the fence as straight as a die, and the ball never deviated an inch from the line. Even that effort left me none too well off, although I did have the easier approach to make because I was nearer the green.

Roger pitched over a trap near the green and his ball hopped on, stopping twenty feet from the cup. I had to win the hole. I played a low flying shot, that landed a few yards from the green and kept going, finally stopping six feet away. Wethered putted and missed, and I holed mine for a three, which placed me one down. Then we came to the terrible seventeenth. This is a par five, but, like the fifteenth, reachable in two. The fact that you can get home in two does not mean a thing, because there are so many dangers trying for the green that it is hardly worth the effort. We had two good tee shots. I played an iron, a safety-first sort of stroke, that could get me to the front edge and no farther. That is where my ball ended. Wethered, who knew the St. Andrews course like a book, deliberately played to the left beyond the little trap guarding the green and onto the eighteenth tee. I did not understand why he should do such a thing, but it did not take me long to find out his reason. When we arrived at our balls, I was left with a nasty approach putt up over a steep incline, a shot I abhor, whereas Roger had a nice place from which to roll his ball to the hole with nothing dangerous in the way. I putted and put my ball eight or ten inches from the cup. Wethered putted again from off the green, got inside, and that hole was halved.

With me now one down, we came to the thirty-sixth hole. The fairway to this hole adjoins the first, and there is nothing in the way of trouble anywhere unless one hits a badly sliced ball. Neither Roger nor I were slicing our tee shots, so this difficulty was eliminated as we drove two tee shots toward the hole. Directly in front of the green, and forming part of it, is a huge undulation four or five feet below the topmost section of the green. This is called the 'Valley of Sin,' because, it is said, the hapless player who places a ball into the Valley of Sin must take at least three putts. The bank is so sheer, one must hit his ball hard enough to get out of it and yet not too hard to roll beyond the green. It tries the soul of everyone who gets into it.

Roger played a fine second twenty feet past the hole. I used a mashie, hit my ball, saw it clear the Valley of Sin, and then was a bit disappointed to see it stop quickly. It went straight for the flag, which was and always is majestically held by that great old veteran Andrew Kirkaldy. Andrew is one of the most famous of the golfing professionals, and no event would be complete unless he held the pin on the last green. It is part of the ceremony. It is Andrew who decides the ball away, and then silence ensues.

Andrew took two glances, one at my ball, the other at Roger's, and signaled to Wethered to putt. My ball was eighteen feet from the hole on the short side, Roger twenty feet beyond on the other. He putted his slippery downhill putt gently, it caught the roll, and slid ominously toward the cup. I waited, it seemed, hours. His ball rolled quietly, slowed down, and died on the very lip. That in itself was bad medicine for me, but to make matters just a trifle more distressing, my path to the hole was blocked by half the diameter of the ball.

I can remember studying the line of my putt and wondering how in the world I could get by his ball and get my own into the hole. Eighteen-foot putts at best give you a headache when there is nothing in the way but the hole, and you have to sink the putt. Well, anyway, as I stood there wondering, the thought occurred to me that I might try to hit his ball. Normally when you try to do something in golf, you fail, and this was my particular psychology. I figured that in trying to hit Roger's ball, mine would miss and perhaps catch the edge of the rim and tumble in. I had to putt to the right, and the upper portion of the hole was shut off. My only hope was to have it drop in from the lower opening. I hit my putt just hard enough to reach his ball, saw it take the break, and then lose its momentum and, as it was dying, it skimmed by and fell in for a three, which squared the match at last. I had played the last three holes three under par, had won two of them, and had equaled the record of the course with a 70. Bobby Jones has since reduced this by two strokes.

Thinking the match had to be finished, I stalked off to the first tee and waited for Roger. Then our referee informed me that the match must end as a tie. That was satisfactory for both of us, and the referee further stated it would be a shame for such a fine match to end any other way than even, which I thought was a most sporting thing for him to say. Looking at the score, I found that Rotan and Marston had won their matches with fair comfort, but Sweetser had been beaten by Tolley and the Britons led by four matches to three, taking into consideration the foursome play of the day before.

Then Bob Gardner came in a one-up winner over Harris, and the sides were deadlocked again. I stood on the veranda of the Grand Hotel as Gardner and Harris reached the eighteenth green. From my position looking down on the green, I saw Bob hit a mean five-foot putt smack into the hole in the most convincing manner imaginable. Fred Wright and Ernest Holderness followed. The last I had heard about this match, Wright was several holes down and apparently beaten. Here they were coming to the last hole. Both on in two, Wright's ball seven feet from the cup. Holderness on a long putt put his ball stone dead. Freddy,

than whom there is not a finer fighter, coldly
sighted his putt, stepped up, and banged that one
in for a three. Then we learned he had been two
down and three to play and had won the last three
holes. That victory put the Americans a match
to the good and there were two left, Herron and the
Scottish schoolmaster, John Wilson, and Doctor
Willing opposed to Willie Murray. Herron, weigh-
ing well over two hundred pounds, was beaten by
Wilson, and the outcome of the Walker Cup de-
pended entirely on the Murray-Willing affair, the
last match of the day. By that time the crowd was
in a frenzy, because they had been looking at golf
of a superlative sort all day long, and it dashed
madly for the seventeenth green to see the final
match.

The two players came along, and the expression
on their faces clearly told of the terrific battle they
were having. By the time the gallery reached a
point near the green, they were shut off, and no
one knew — that is, those about the green — how
the players stood. Carefully they approached the
treacherous putting surface. Murray was away,
and from twenty feet he grazed the hole. The good
Doctor, a brilliant putter, was ten feet from the
cup. Doctor Willing leaves nothing to chance on a
putting green and took plenty of time. He examined the line of putt from in back of the hole and
from behind his ball. He walked down one side and

up the other. He even looked into the hole — I suppose to see if it was really there. In any event, when he got ready, he putted and holed it. Then he turned to Willie Murray, who was walking toward him with hand outstretched in congratulation to the winner. It was, indeed, a happy band of American golfers who gathered in their livingroom that evening to talk over the doings of the day. There may be closer Walker Cup matches than that, but they will not happen often. The total score was America six, Great Britain five, with one match a tie, and the Walker Cup was brought home. It may appear that I have dwelt too long on this contest, but it is impossible to do full justice in fewer words.

Coming back to the United States, the first event of importance was the open championship. It was played at Inwood, Long Island, a very fine but difficult golf course. I had not been a regular contender for this championship, but I decided to take it in, and Bobby Jones and I got a room at the clubhouse and lived together. There is little to report of my own activities because the course was too severe for me the way I was playing. I had the pleasure, however, of playing with John Black, the grand old Scotchman, who came within a hair of winning the 1922 open, and also with McDonald Smith.

In the morning of the first round with Black, an

136

interesting and amusing thing happened. John had built up a neat score for the first nine. The tenth hole at Inwood was an elbow, calling for a tee shot to the right and then a mashie niblick pitch to a very narrow green studded with traps. It sounds easy to say a drive to the right, but the real trouble is on the left of the fairway and must be avoided. Further, near the green on the left in 1923 were several oak trees, one of which was quite prominent. John drove and pulled his ball into a trap. It stopped in that deadly stuff called beach grass. He was barely able to knock it out of this lie to the bottom of a trap in front. Now seventy-five yards from the green, in a trap, having already played two, John had nothing in the way but another trap near the green and that high and sturdy oak. Never have I seen a more hopeless prospect. John scowled a few times, took a look at the situation, another at his ball, hit it, and saw it come out and up as clean as a whistle. It cleared the tree, landed on the green, and rolled into the cup for a three! That was certainly turning a seven into a hole done in better than par figures.

McDonald Smith was not at his best and did not figure in the championship to any great extent. While he and I were delayed on the short twelfth tee, we were amused at Joe Kirkwood doing some of his stunts on the side. This hole measured about a hundred and ten yards and had to be played over

137

a water hazard. Joe was busy pitching balls into his caddie's pocket with unerring accuracy, and finally it came time for him to play. After the exhibition he had given, everybody expected a pitch stone dead to the flag. Instead, Kirkwood lifted his head like the veriest duffer and popped his ball into the middle of the pond.

My roommate Bobby was giving a very fine account of himself, and, deprived of winning amateur and open championships until that year, he had thrown his hat into the ring in earnest. Inwood, as I have already stated, was cruelly difficult. There was not the least semblance of what could be called a resting hole, and the golfer had to be keyed up to the highest pitch at all times. The course gave away nothing, and low scores had to be earned.

With the title practically sewed up, Bobby pulled a second shot to the left of the eighteenth green in short rough. The green was roped off, and Bobby's second was just outside of the roped area. He had a perfect right to have the ropes removed, but he thought he could pitch his ball under and have it go onto the green. The ball came up too quickly, hit the rope, and bounded back. Then he did remove the ropes. He played his fourth on, and with two putts holed out in six, which gave him a seventy-two total of 296, six strokes ahead of the nearest player. An average of 74's seemed unbeatable. Then word came back that Cruikshank needed only par figures on the last three holes to tie Jones.

Cruikshank was putting on the sixteenth green. He had a putt of not over two feet for his par four on that hole. Carelessly he putted and missed, and his chances seemed nil. He got his four on seventeen, but he had to do a three on the eighteenth to tie. That eighteenth hole at Inwood is one of the last holes in the world that I should select if I wanted to get a three. The hole calls for a long tee shot — long so that the player can have ample leeway to play over a lagoon to the green. It is well beyond the four-hundred-yard mark in length. Cruikshank got his long tee shot, and then planted a gorgeous iron six feet from the hole. The crowd roared. It was no trick at all for Cruikshank to hole the putt, and he and Jones were in a tie for the championship.

Bobby Jones felt very blue. He could not get over his exhibition on the eighteenth, but a ride in Tom Logan's car to the Engineers' Club at Roslyn, where we had dinner, caused him to dismiss his worries, for the time being at least. We got back to Inwood, and retired early.

Many people wonder what a golfer does at night while he is waiting for the time to arrive for a play-off. In Bobby Jones's case, he got a book, read a few chapters, and turned in for a fine night of rest.

The tie was to be played on Sunday afternoon, and the crowd gathered early. I appointed myself a policeman, to keep well-wishing friends away from Bobby, because one of the most tiring things in the world is to talk golf just before a big match. Several people came to our room, the door of which was locked, and only Bobby's closest friends succeeded in getting through the guard.

The scoring was close all the way, never more than one stroke separating the pair. As a body-guard, Jones had his old friend Tom Paine as head marshal, and Tommy Logan and I acted as assistants, our main duties being to keep spectators from bothering him and upsetting his concentration. Playing the eighteenth, Jones was a stroke to the good. He hit a long tee shot down the right-hand side of the fairway, in the face of a stiff breeze, and his ball stopped in the rough just off the fairway. Cruikshank missed his drive so badly, he could not play for the green, and his second fell short of the lagoon.

Bobby Jones's ball was not lying well, and those of us who stood near him wondered just what sort of shot he would attempt under the conditions. In front of the green was that awe-inspiring lagoon of water, and if he failed to carry this, there was no telling what might happen. He was laboring under a terrific mental strain, and I shuddered as he chose a driving iron, the hardest club in the bag to play. He took his stance and I closed my eyes. I heard the iron meet the ball, looked up, and saw the ball flying like an arrow right for the flag. It cleared the water by a safe enough margin and rolled within six feet of the hole. It was the finest shot I had ever seen, taking into consideration the lie of the ball, the club selected, and the distance. That shot, of course, settled the title beyond any further doubt, and it proved to be the first of the many major championships that Bobby won. He was naturally delighted beyond words, because he had struggled year after year without luck to get to the top of the heap and at last his perseverance was rewarded.

CHAPTER IX

A YOUTH FROM ATLANTA

GOOD golfers, with the proper amount of determination plus a sound game, cannot be denied forever. Bobby Jones proved this at Inwood. Another, who had had his fair share and more, too, of golfing misfortunes, was to come into his own after a long quest for high honors. This was Max Marston in the amateur championship played at Flossmoor several weeks after the open. Naturally, Bobby Jones was the favorite, but he had not established himself as a match player, although I always believed the golfer capable of turning in fine medal scores must develop sooner or later into a successful match player.

The qualifying medal contest resulted in a tie between Chick Evans and Bobby Jones, at 149, an unusually low total for that long and testing course. About the only thing that could be classified as a spectacular performance in that qualifying round was the play of Jesse Guilford on the home hole. Jesse was in plenty of trouble and faced the necessity of having to make a four, one under par, on the long eighteenth to get into the match-play rounds. The hole measured about five hundred and fifty yards, and very few players were reaching the green in two. Guilford, realizing his plight, put

142

everything he had into his tee shot and hit a tremendous drive down the fairway. There was quite a roll from right to left, and he deliberately played up the slope on his second. On the upper corner of the green was a trap.

Big Jesse had every reason to expect his ball to kick to the left almost immediately after it landed, but he hit his ball so well and it had so much power behind it that it bounded forward into the trap. Given the proper sort of break, it would have been on the green and not far from the cup, where a four would have been simple. Those two shots, the drive and brassie, were as fine as any two successive shots could possibly be, and yet his ball was resting in the bottom of a shallow sand trap, with the green falling rapidly away. His only chance now to qualify was to place his ball dead out of the little pit. He used a putter, rolling the ball up the sandy bank. It slowed up a bit and then continued to roll down the slope and into the hole for a three, two better than par. It was a grand recovery, and the Siege Gun was immensely pleased.

I got by my first two matches, the first against Tony Haines, the old Yale football player, and Willie Hunter, the British chap, who had taken up residence in California.

The big surprise of the early rounds was the defeat of Bobby Jones in the second round. Max Marston, his opponent, played thirty-five holes in several strokes better than par and his play was positively invincible.

An interesting thing occurred in the first round in the match between Eddie Held and Densmore Shute. It was a thirty-six-hole match, and at the end of fourteen holes, Held was four up. Shute, who has since turned professional and is one of the best golfers in the country, won three successive holes. Playing the eighteenth, he was one down. He had a putt of ten feet to square the match. With due care he putted his ball and, just as it appeared as though it must go in, it turned away and stayed out. The hole was halved and Shute offered his hand as a token of congratulation. Eddie said, 'This is a thirty-six-hole match.' Shute had thought he was beaten. In the afternoon he went out and beat Held.

My third-round match with George Von Elm was one of those tough, close contests. In the morning I was one up. Such a lead is little or nothing against a man of Von Elm's ability, and I knew I had a battle on my hands. We fought back and forth, with the lead shifting from one to the other, until I finally stood on the fifteenth tee one hole to the good. I pulled my ball badly off the tee and it landed in the rough and among some trees. The hole was a hard par four, and there was plenty of trouble along the way, particularly in front of the green, where a big water ditch crossed

144

the fairway. Von Elm had an excellent opportunity of squaring the match by hitting his tee shot straight. Instead of doing this, he pulled his ball into deeper rough than mine and there was little to choose in the matter of advantage. Von Elm played first and contented himself with playing safely to the fairway, a few yards from his ball. I observed the location of his ball in the fairway and knew he had left himself a very long iron to the green. I decided to play as close to the water ditch as possible, because by so doing I should have a short pitch left for the green. With a mashie I hit the ball, and it fell thirty yards short of the water hazard and about eighty yards from the green.

Now it was up to Von Elm. He was at least a hundred and eighty yards away and had a difficult stroke to play, but to his credit he played it twenty feet from the hole. I had been playing my pitch shots well with my mashie niblick and the only thing I had to make sure of doing was to keep my eye on the ball. I could see the flag, but the view to the green was shut off by a willow that grew out of the water. I looked at the ball carefully, hit it over the small tree, and knew it was somewhere on the green. As we crossed the bridge and the green opened up, my ball was seen ten inches from the cup. I won the hole. The next two holes being halved, I passed into the semi-finals.

Gardner was to play Sweetser, the defender in the upper half, and my opponent was Max Marston. Sweetser had little trouble with Gardner and beat him eight and seven. My match with Max was one of those gnawing affairs where one and then the other was leading, but never by any great margin. At the twenty-seventh hole I was one down. It seemed as though I should never be able to square the match, because Marston was playing inspired golf, and when it did appear as though I might win a hole, he would lay an approach dead or else sink a long putt. The tenth was an excellent example of what I was up against. This hole, slightly downhill, measured four hundred and eighty yards, but was reachable with two good shots. We hit long and straight tee shots. Max, playing his second before me, pushed off line to the deep rough on the right. I banged a long spoon shot, all carry to the green, and the ball bit the soft turf and stopped almost immediately twelve feet from the hole. I had every reason to think I should at last even our match.

Max stepped into the long grass with his niblick, took a swing, hit his ball up in the air, and it traveled on toward the flag, eventually stopping eight inches from the cup. I could not get my putt and the hole was halved. So was the short eleventh. We both played to the twelfth rather cautiously, because the slightest error on the way meant a lost hole for one or the other. I could ill-afford to lose the hole and Marston wished to protect his lead. However, I did have an eighteen-footer for a win and luckily holed it, and the match was square.

Then things happened. The thirteenth hole at Flossmoor was a very short one, calling for a mashie niblick pitch. The green sloped abruptly from right to left, and ordinarily the player tries to place his ball on the upper part, allowing for the slope to turn his ball toward the center of the green. The day Max and I played, the pin was placed on the lower section of the green. On the left-hand corner was a young walnut tree not more than twenty-five or thirty feet in height, and a few feet beyond was the hole. As we stood on the tee, the tree was almost in line with the flag.

There was no rule then about ribbed or punched clubs, and I had a mashie niblick that was punched so heavily its face resembled a rasp. The club had served me well. On soggy or clovery fairways this club gripped the ball beautifully and imparted a tremendous amount of backspin. I made up my mind to blaze away at the flag, disregarding the tree, the roll of the green, and every other thing. I knew if my ball landed on the green, it would stay. I hit the ball firmly, watched it climb, saw it clear the tree, and strike five feet beyond the pin and hop back toward the cup. That shot gave me as much pleasure as any shot I had ever played,

147

taking into consideration the closeness of the match and the chance I had gambled with. Marston was not so successful. He did not hit what was for him a good shot, although his ball stopped on the upper edge of the green a full fifty feet from the hole. He had left himself a nasty downhill putt on a slippery green.

I have always made it a practice to assume that my opponent will play a perfect shot, for the reason that if he does the unusual, I am not shaken too badly mentally. I placed myself for the moment in Max's position and did my best to concede him everything. The best conclusion I could possibly arrive at was that Marston would lay his putt dead for a three. To do this he must make a phenomenal putt. Then I turned to study my own putt of four feet. There was quite a roll, and I had to borrow at least six inches. Still my ball was only four feet away and I had been putting well. The worst I could possibly get was a half. All these thoughts were running through my mind.

Then I turned and watched Max. He had taken his stance and putted. I watched his ball roll gently over the lightning-fast surface down the incline. Yes, it would be dead. I looked my line over again. My putt seemed a bit easier the second glance. As I stood in back of my ball, I turned my head just in time to see my opponent's ball drop into the hole for a two. Max had accomplished a miracle. And instead of having a four-foot curving putt for a win, my ball seemed to be ten feet away and the roll seemed to be twice as severe. The shock was too great; I missed. Now one up, Marston walked away from me, and with two more fine putts the match ended in his favor three up and two to play. He was deserving of his victory.

The next day he beat Jesse Sweetser in a great thirty-eight-hole final, and Max Marston was crowned the champion after years of as hard luck as any champion ever experienced. Sweetser was striving to make it two straight titles, and the last three holes of their match were quite dramatic. On the thirty-sixth green, Sweetser holed a mean six-footer around Marston's ball to keep the match alive. On the thirty-seventh, Sweetser, with a splendid opportunity to win, put a long iron into a trap guarding the green, and the hole was halved. Playing the hundred and eighty or ninety yard second, the thirty-eighth hole of the match, Max hit his iron to the middle of the green. Sweetser pushed his off line to the rough and then made a brilliant recovery to within eight feet of the cup. He still had a chance. Marston always has been a marvelous putter, and on this occasion he stroked his ball to the very edge of the hole rim and completely shut off whatever chances Sweetser might have by laying him a dead stymie. That ended the championship of 1923.

From that year on, or rather I should say that beginning 1924, Bobby Jones was the dominating character in American golf until his retirement in the fall of 1930. In 1924 he won his first national amateur championship at Merion, and the ease with which he walked through the field was astonishing, because there were many fine amateurs in that competition. The field was given a touch of high life in the second qualification test when Clarke Corkran did the most amazing scoring imaginable when he waltzed around the difficult Merion layout in 67. Such scoring seems unbelievable, but 'Ducky' Corkran is one of those fellows who do the impossible.

Apart from Jones's brilliant golf there were several notable contests. Roland McKenzie, the smooth-swinging Washington, D.C., player, found himself eight down and fifteen to play against George Von Elm, certainly a hopeless predicament. No one gave that match a thought after the morning round. Then word sifted back to the clubhouse to the effect that McKenzie was putting up a glorious battle. He won back seven of the eight holes, and was now but one down and one to play. If there is one shot necessary on the eighteenth hole at Merion, it is a long straight drive. McKenzie skied his ball so badly he did not get out of the rough. Von Elm was far down the middle with an iron left for the green. Standing with one foot well below the other, Roland smashed a mighty spoon shot from the rough two hundred and seventy-five yards to the green, all carry, and won the hole, to square the match. The battle he had put up softened him for the extra hole, for with a putt of not more than twelve feet he three-putted and was beaten.

I had two interesting matches that I like to remember. The first was against my friend Jesse Guilford. In the morning round we played like a couple of duffers, and I doubt if either of us broke 90. We gabbed and chatted in a manner that indicated that we were not the least bit concerned as to the outcome, and neither did we care. We had many things in common to discuss on the way and our concentration was at a very low ebb. We got together at luncheon and agreed to play as well as we could and try to beat the tar out of the other fellow. It has always been difficult for me to play seriously, especially when competing against an old team mate.

In the afternoon we went at one another in a dog-eat-dog fashion. The match was square at the third. The fourth was a three-shotter. I played a short pitch over the brook guarding the green Guilford popped his into the water. He took a penalty stroke and chipped his ball eight feet from the hole. That was his fifth and I had two putts for the win. I putted stone dead and withdrew for

Guilford to play. He looked at me in surprise. I had forgotten that he lay five. He walked away toward the next tee. I said, 'Wait a minute, I am not conceding you that putt.' He smiled and said, 'That's all right with me, but I am giving you the hole.' I went on to win from Jesse by four and three.

Another match that stands out in my memory was the one I had with Willie Hunter. It was at thirty-six holes. Three times I had worked myself into the rather comfortable lead of five holes. The last time I was five up and ten to play, and then the tide came in on me. Hunter won three holes in a row and then another. With three holes left, I was only one up. Hunter drove as straight as a die down the fairway. I hooked my ball badly and found it under a low-hanging rum-cherry tree in the rough. The second shot from the fairway had to be played over a quarry and I did not have a burglar's chance of hitting my ball toward the green. I could not afford to lose the hole, and still I did not see any chance of preventing such a calamity. I could play out to the fairway ahead of Hunter's ball. That would give him quite an advantage because he could bang away with a mashie or light iron, knowing that the best I could possibly do would be to reach the green in three. Therefore, I deliberately played out to a position short of his ball which meant that I must play three before he played his second. I did this because I had a hunch I could place my ball within putting distance. I stepped up to my ball after getting it back onto the fairway and hit a mashie shot four feet from the pin from a distance of about a hundred and fifty yards. Hunter was somewhat disturbed at this sudden turn of affairs and failed to carry the quarry, and a hole that seemed irretrievably gone fell into my lap. We halved the seventeenth and the match was over. I had worked myself into the semi-finals there to play Bobby Jones. What Bobby did to me was criminal. He was unbeatable, and made the winning of holes by me so impossible that I was soundly trounced eleven up and ten to play.

The next day he showed George Von Elm little or no mercy and became the amateur title-holder for the first time in his career. That championship made a new man out of Bobby Jones. He had definitely established himself as a golfer long before and his scoring in medal competition was the acme of consistency. In match play he had not enjoyed the success his great game justified. If he had a weakness at all in this style of play, it was that of playing the man shot for shot and frequently he was on the losing end simply because he tried to play the man and not the hole. In our semi-final match he disregarded my play entirely and played against the par of the course.

It is far better for a star golfer in a match-play

game to forget his physical opponent and compete with the par on the holes as they come along. Any golfer capable of playing par golf is not losing to the ideal score many holes, and this system is bound to win in the long run, excepting, to be sure, those rare occasions where the opponent himself is improving upon par, in which case defeats are bound to occur.

I have always felt that any golfer who had the ability to score low in medal competition should be able to do so in match-play contests, and Bobby Jones's first success at Merion in 1924 convinced me that my reasoning was correct. The successful match player learns much through experiences gained in hard matches, and the fact that Bobby had not been successful up to that year did not necessarily mean that he lacked match-play ability. In an earlier chapter I pointed out the success of Jerry Travers at match play and how he won the open championship of 1915, though admittedly an inferior medal scorer.

When the open championship was awarded to the Worcester Country Club in 1925, I decided to have a go at it. Medal tournaments and open championships had lost their attraction for me and I was an infrequent attendant in score-play events. First of all, I dislike that form of play, because the player must play cautiously or carefully, and I prefer to speculate with my shots, taking long risks to win or lose holes. Medal play represents the better test, but to me it lacks the zest and pleasure of a close match. But Worcester was near home and I liked the course, and consequently entered the championship.

A qualifying test was held at Lido for the Eastern delegation, and Lido, situated at Long Beach, Long Island, is one of the fine courses of the world. McDonald Smith had two beautiful rounds of 70 to lead his section of the field and Bobby Jones was winner in his half. I had two steady rounds of 75 and 76, which qualified me safely, and on to Worcester the qualifiers trooped. The thermometer ranged between ninety and a hundred the two days we played, and the heat proved too much for McDonald Smith and Tommy Armour as well as several other splendid players.

The first day, or rather the first round, I had the pleasure of leading the entire field with a 70. To do this I holed a putt of at least forty feet downhill, reminiscent of the one Marston holed against me at Flossmoor, and I can truthfully say I should have been delighted to have got down in two putts from where my ball lay. My partner was Gene Sarazen and he played brilliantly after a slow start. Two things stand out in our afternoon round that I shall never forget. Golfers who are inclined to lose heart after badly played shots should take a lesson from Gene Sarazen and bear in mind that, because a ball has been badly played, it does not necessarily indicate that all hope is gone. Gene stood on the first tee and topped his ball. He was very much in the running for the title and, though three rounds remained to be played, he was not helping his cause any by topping his tee shot. The hole calls for a drive and mashie. Sarazen wasted his drive and had to do some clever playing to get a five, one above par. He knocked his second with a spoon over the brook, pitched to the green fifteen feet from the hole, and then sank the putt for a par four. I had played the hole perfectly, but got no better than four.

Then we came to the long second. With a drive and brassie I was just short of the putting surface in two, chipped on, and got a par five. Sarazen sliced his drive to the rough, recovered to the rough on the left, was still in the rough to the left of the green in three, and forthwith chipped into the hole for a better-than-par four. Anything can happen in this bally game.

Willie MacFarlane, always a grand player, astounded the Worcester galleries by romping around in 67, establishing a new record for the course and incidentally taking the lead at the halfway mark. Bobby Jones, with a mediocre opening round of 77, hit a fast streak and pulled himself up with the leaders with a splendid 70. The scoring was low in spite of the heat, and at the end of fifty-four holes six or eight men had an excellent shot at the title. I was three strokes behind the leader, Willie Mac-Farlane, and one ahead of Bobby Jones.

A brisk wind had sprung up as I teed my ball for the last round and, striving too hard to make the proper wind allowance, I pulled my tee shot to the rough and directly behind a large elm tree. My ball was teed up in the long grass and I was undecided whether to play back to the fairway or take a shot at the green. I wanted a four badly. There was just room enough to hit a low iron under an overhanging branch and I took the gamble. The ball came out all right, but instead of flying below the branch it caught it full on, with the result that I not only failed to reach the green, but I ended up with a six, which put me in a bad way. The next hole was well over five hundred yards and I had the wind in back of me. For three successive rounds I had been quite close to the green with no helping wind, and this time I went out for everything. I have never hit two finer shots in succession. The drive traveled two hundred and seventy yards and the brassie was just as long, and my ball was actually on the green in two. Here was an excellent chance of recovering a valuable stroke. But — the approach putt was weak, and, missing the six-footer, I gained nothing.

Then we came to the one-shooter, the fourth. I had played this hole in fours twice and five once, thereby losing four strokes to par. I banged a brassie to the back edge of the green and then took three to hole out. On the four rounds I not only had failed to make a single par three, but had averaged worse than four. It was not a particularly difficult hole, but it proved my Nemesis. Willie MacFarlane also had his troubles on that very same hole and his scores were the same as my own.

From there on, things rolled along on an even keel until I struck the short tenth. A spade mashie pitch left me an eight-foot putt for a two. I had been putting splendidly, but with no success, and time and time again many putts that looked as good as gold as they left the putter curled around the cup and remained out. I felt I needed that two to win and, forgetting the speed of the green, I putted so firmly my ball rolled over the hold and five feet beyond. Again I missed the five-footer. Even with all these errors, my golf in between was sound and, standing on the sixteenth tee, I needed three fours to tie the leaders, MacFarlane and Jones. The tee shot on the sixteenth was one that required accuracy above all things, because the fairway was carved through the woods that bordered both sides. When I hammered a long ball right down the middle, I was confident I could get a four. The green sloped away toward the back, and I debated as to whether I should play a running shot or pitch all the way to the green, depending upon the backspin to hold the ball there. I elected to pitch, and then committed an unpardonable golfing sin.

Once your mind is made up to play a certain stroke, you should go through with it. I took my stance with a mashie niblick in my hand, got the club halfway back, and then in the middle of the swing I suddenly decided to play a pitch and run. That was fatal. I turned the face of the club over on the ball as I came in contact with it and a badly pulled shot to the rough on the left resulted. That finished my hopes then and there, for I failed to chip dead and had to be satisfied with a five. Four poorly played holes cost me that championship, but then Bobby Jones and Willie MacFarlane undoubtedly could recall many similar slips in the progress of their play. As it was, I finished one stroke behind the pair in a tie with Johnny Farrell for third and fourth positions.

On Friday, June 5, 1925, Willie MacFarlane and Jones met at the Worcester Country Club under a broiling sun, with the temperature somewhere around ninety-five, to decide which would be the open champion. Jones was the favorite, and after a morning of very even play, it was MacFarlane who had the better chance. They were even in the number of strokes taken at the end of seventeen holes, and when Willie pitched a glorious shot four feet from the cup on the final hole, I do believe Bobby really hoped he would sink it, and thus put a finish to that hot week of golf. It was not to be, however, for Willie missed that putt, and they had to play another eighteen holes that afternoon.

Jones appeared to be thoroughly worn out, and MacFarlane looked as cool as a cucumber. Bobby played a great nine holes, going out in 35 to MacFarlane's 39, and you would not have given a nickel for the latter's chances. One by one the strokes came back through spectacular iron work assisted by brilliant putting, and an incoming nine of 33 turned the trick in favor of Willie. He had accomplished a feat that seemed impossible, that of outplaying Jones five strokes on a nine-hole stretch. Again there is nothing that cannot happen in golf.

CHAPTER X

SWEETSER AT MUIRFIELD

THE venue for the amateur championship of that
same year was Oakmont, and, in order to bring the
field down to a less unwieldy group for the match-
play rounds, a thirty-six-hole medal test was arranged, the sixteen low scorers qualifying for the
championship. On any course that was not too
difficult, this might have been successful, but Oakmont is one of those devastating layouts where
eights and nines crop up with alarming regularity,
and the knowledge of but sixteen open places does
not help the golfer's mentality in the least when he
is trying to escape traps and three-putt greens.

That championship was a nightmare in so far as
the qualifying round was concerned. You could not
figure on a thing, and there was just one thought in
the mind of everybody, and that was to get through
with the thirty-six holes and hope the total amassed
was low enough to survive the match-play schedule. Seven of us tied at 158 for five places, and
away we started for the play-off. My drive was hit
to the left and caught a trap, the ball stopping
smack against a steep embankment. When it came
my turn to play, I chose a niblick and tried merely
to get my ball out on the fairway for a shot at the

green, because I was reasonably certain a five would do some good. I did not try for a spectacular recovery, because the risk was too great and there was nothing to be gained. I might just as well have tried to plug that niblick shot two hundred to the green, because I failed dismally to get it onto the fairway. From then it was a struggle which terminated in my failure to qualify. I had never been caught in the snare of a qualifying play-off before, and I wish to state now, I would prefer failure to qualify any time to a play-off, where players are made to suffer while spectators revel in the ordeal. But then it is only a game, and after all I do not feel as bitter as I may sound. Nevertheless, play-offs are dreadful things, and I feel sorry for those who have to submit to them.

Watts Gunn, making his initial appearance at an amateur meeting, played and defeated Jesse Sweetser in the second round ten up and nine to play. He was naturally elated, so pleased, in fact, that he asked Bobby Jones whether or not Bobby did not think that Watts should wire his father the details. 'That is not necessary,' said Jones. 'Your father knows that already. Nevertheless, Watts was delighted beyond words, and eventually reached the finals, where he had to play his friend and adviser, Bobby Jones. He made a real match out of it, too, for a long time, but Bobby, somewhat disturbed at the persistency of Watts, let out a few notches and knocked him out by eight up and seven to play. Nevertheless, reaching the finals in his first championship was quite an achievement, and Watts deserved plenty of credit.

In 1904, Walter J. Travis went to England quietly, and after several weeks of preparation visited Sandwich and then walked off with the British amateur championship. Since that time there had been many American golfers who had tried to duplicate Travis's performance, but none had ever succeeded. Some came close to the goal, but they could not quite break through. A very strong team of golfers went abroad in 1926, and two objectives were in mind: first, the British amateur championship, and then the Walker Cup contest. The championship was to be played at Muirfield, thirty miles or so from Edinburgh, and we were anxious for one of our players to win if possible.

Led by Bobby Jones, the team consisted of the Walker Cup captain, Bob Gardner, Jesse Guilford, Sweetser, Gunn, McKenzie, Von Elm, and myself. Chick Evans was also a visitor, but he had gone over on his own account and was not included on the American Walker Cup team. Two days out of New York, Sweetser contracted sinus trouble, and he was affected throughout the trip with this miserable disease. Otherwise, every American was playing fine golf and prepared to put up the battle of his life to take out this player or that on the way to the title. Sweetser was too ill to indulge in the many practice rounds that were arranged, and his chances were considered lightly as the day approached for the event.

A British championship meeting is an intensely interesting affair, and it takes two or three days of play to get the field into a condition where one can tell who his next-round opponent is to be. It is not at all unusual to have two hundred or more entries, and the wonderful thing to me is how the draw can be arranged so accurately as to have two players left at the end of the week. There is no qualifying round, but the powers that be have every little detail worked out carefully and it comes out perfectly in the end.

In the early rounds the draw was particularly unkind. For example, Von Elm and I, after winning our first matches, had to play one another in the second round. I managed to beat George three up and two to play in a match that was close all the way. Playing the short thirteenth, I led by a hole. The green is hemmed in on the left and in back by a huge sand dune that serves as an excellent vantage-point for spectators who wish to see as much play as possible with a minimum of effort. I half-topped a spade mashie shot and the ball sped on a line for the bank in back. It struck high up on the dune, hesitated a second, and then rolled back onto the green twenty-five feet from the hole. It was a terrible shot. Von Elm, on the other hand, hit a beauty six feet from the hole, and it looked good all the way. I felt inwardly ashamed, but my ball was on the green and there was nothing else to do but putt it at the hole. In it went for a two, and I can still see the look of disgust and surprise on George's face. He holed out also, but he chided me good-naturedly for my piece of fortune. After all, golfers are human even when the luck goes against them.

Bobby Jones was playing the finest golf imaginable when he took the tee against the champion Robert Harris, and he proceeded to burn up the course with a steady stream of threes and fours. He overwhelmed Harris, a very steady and sound golfer, by a margin of eight up and seven to play, and when the match ended, Jones was something like five under fours for the eleven holes played. Jones was at the crest of his best game, and the British amateur title in the opinion of many was as good as his. His play was invincible. The difficult thing about the game of golf is reaching the peak and then trying to stay there. No man living could have beaten Jones the day he played Bob Harris.

The very next morning he was drawn against a young Scot named Andrew Jamieson. There are many fine players scattered throughout the British Isles and little is known of their ability except locally. Jamieson was one of these. He was well known around Edinburgh, but that was all. He had had no real testing in the crucible of competition, and therefore in the eyes of everyone it was just another golf match for Bobby Jones on his way to the finals. Usually after an extraordinary round, the player softens up a bit in his play and it becomes ragged. Jones cracked two fine shots to the edge of the first green and then, to the surprise of all, including Jamieson, took three putts. A hole or two later, he passed up another chance to win a hole by making a mistake. Badly outdriven all the way, Jamieson was doing a masterly job with his chipping iron and putter, and at the turn had a two-hole lead. He was far short of the tenth green in two, but with a deadly chip and one putt he halved the hole. Jones could not get going at all, and became three down. And finally four down with four to go. Jamieson, with victory in sight and the hooks well set, halved the fifteenth to win the match. Bobby had no excuses to offer, because there were none, but it is a fact that he never won a single hole from Jamieson.

Meanwhile, the weakened and fever-stricken Sweetser was winning close matches and having a hard time of it. We came together in the third round, and I had him two down at the ninth. I hit a fine drive from the tenth tee, and when he got his ball heavily and reached the rough on the right, I had every reason to think I might win that hole. Sweetser could not possibly get the green with his

second, and, indeed, it was doubtful whether or not
he could carry a deep cross-trap placed to catch a
missed shot. Jesse realized his predicament and
tried to clear the trap. The ball was hit solidly, but
the long grass pulled it down, and it landed in the
sand, but with sufficient power behind it to roll
through the sand and onto the grass bank. My
second, played with a number two iron, struck
short of the green and rolled to the back edge.
Sweetser climbed up the embankment and then
played a high pitch of a hundred and twenty-five
yards fifteen feet from the hole. In all probability
two putts would give me a win, and since I was
putting downhill on a fast surface, I made sure to
putt beyond the cup so as to leave myself an up-
hiller for the four. Sweetser, also above the hole,
had a mean curling putt for his four, and the odds
were distinctly in my favor. My approach putt
was hit just a trifle too firmly and it skidded past
eight feet. It is not always possible to lay fifty-foot
putts dead on fast greens and my effort was satisfactory, taking everything into consideration.
Then I got a shock that was staggering. Sweetser
holed his fifteen-footer, I missed, and a hole that
looked like mine suddenly went the other way.
Now one up, the lead was wiped out completely on
the eleventh, when Jesse poked a long pitch two
feet from the cup.

We battled away on even terms until we reached

the eighteenth. This hole, if my memory serves me, measures four hundred and thirty or forty yards, and is a grand finisher. On the right-hand side of the fairway, just beyond the two-hundred-yard marker, is a sand pit. The wind was blowing from the right, and Jesse started his tee shot for the trap. It never wavered an inch, cleared the pit, and continued on down the fairway. I followed suit, hit my ball well, but it caught the top of the pit and rolled back into the sand. There was nothing to do but play out and hope a five would save me. I did make a five, but it might just as well have been a ten for all the good it did. Sweetser hit a long iron that covered the flag all the way and stopped ten feet from the hole.

Match after match, Sweetser came to that same eighteenth hole either square with his opponent or obliged to protect a one-hole lead with a great iron, and he never failed. He had the faculty of playing a wonderful shot when he needed it most, and the feature of his play from every angle was his marvelous courage. His system could retain nothing more than a mouthful of orange juice, and yet he plugged on without complaint, winning matches on the seventeenth or eighteenth greens in spite of his physical weakness. He had won five or six close matches by the time he reached the semi-finals, and in no one of them did he have an easy time.

His opponent in the semi-final round was the

Honorable William Brownlow, a high-ranking golfer. For once Sweetser opened up a lead of two holes and clung to it for dear life, though he could not increase the margin. With two holes remaining, he was dormie up. The seventeenth hole at Muirfield is a long one, with no particular difficulty to overcome on the tee shot. Brownlow, while not an abnormally long driver, had had the best of the driving up to that time in so far as distance was concerned, but it was obvious that Sweetser was holding himself back as much as possible and was gaining length only on those holes where distance was essential. He seemed to sense that distance was necessary on that seventeenth, because he hit a tee shot that traveled close to three hundred yards with a following wind. Brownlow hit his ball seemingly as well, but was fully forty yards behind. He was left with a long shot to carry a deep cross-bunker or else play short. Brownlow chose to go for the carry, hit a nice brassie, but it failed by an eyelash, his ball catching the top and rolling backward a foot or two. Sweetser sized up the situation carefully, and, though he was within range of the green with a brassie, he decided to play safe with an iron.

If there is one shot that Sweetser can play, it is a long iron. He met the ball perfectly and it cleared the trap by fifty yards rolling on toward the green. His second shot could not have been more than

thirty yards from the putting surface and directly
in front of the opening with absolutely nothing between his ball and the hole. I thought at the time
he showed excellent judgment, and now I was sure
of it. Brownlow made a great recovery to the front
edge of the green, but when Jesse approached
twelve feet from the goal, it seemed as though nothing could stop him. Brownlow had been using an
iron putter of the cleek variety and using it well.
For some unknown reason he shifted to a putter of
wood, one of those huge-headed things. He was all
of forty-five feet from the cup, and the odds must
have been a thousand to one against him. Furthermore, he was two down, and the end seemed at
hand. Brownlow, however, had plenty of courage,
and he deliberately looked the line of his putt as
carefully as though it was a simple three-footer.
With a slow backswing he hit his ball smoothly and
it rolled and rolled — Ten, fifteen, twenty feet it
rolled; Twenty-five and thirty. Sweetser was sitting on the green waiting for his opponent's ball to
stop before making his own putt. On came the ball.
It was now headed as straight as a die for the bottom of the tin. It never swerved, never left the
line, and dropped amidst a deafening outbreak of
applause. It was evident the outburst was merely a
recognition of appreciation to a game and fighting
golfer, because it subsided almost as quickly as it
was given. Sweetser had not been putting well, and

now had to sink his twelve-footer to win a match that had seemed already won. He missed, and the pair, the dog-tired Sweetser and the brave young Briton, staggered off to the last teeing ground.

Once again Sweetser drove a long straight tee shot down the middle a full thirty yards in front of his opponent. Brownlow had to play a wooden club of some sort, and, choosing his spoon, he rapped the ball on a line for the pin. It stopped thirty feet past the flag. Jesse had been shooting faultless iron shots at that green ever since the championship started, and on this occasion he delivered still another and well inside the effort of Brownlow's. It was silly to think Brownlow could drop another Herculean putt, and, from every point of view possible to the imagination, this match was to end on the last hole in favor of the sole remaining American, Jesse Sweetser.

Brownlow plucked his wooden putter from the bag, looked the line of his ball over with due care, and took his stance. He had an ugly putt to play. Sweetser, on the other hand, was hole-high on a nice flat piece of putting green. The Englishman tapped his putt gently; it made the roll on the left perfectly; it turned slightly to the right, and then continued along until the hole stopped it. I could not believe my eyes. It seemed impossible for anybody to hole two such putts in succession, but that is what Brownlow did. Poor Jesse. It seemed as if

the Fates had conspired against his winning. He
made a brave but futile effort, as he did on the
seventeenth, but each time his ball only caught a
piece of the hole and stayed out.

The shoe was now on the other foot. Sweetser
was all but out on his feet, but his nerve and courage were still strong as he followed a fine tee shot on
the part of his opponent to the extra hole with one
fully as good. Sweetser was away and he brought
grief to the hearts of his American friends by shov-
ing his spoon shot to a trap short and to the right of
the green. Brownlow, wearing the flush of victory,
played an accurate spoon that placed his ball on
the green a foot or two and thirty feet from the
hole. That settled the match beyond a doubt; but
wait. Sweetser's ball lay under a steep bank in the
sand, and he might explode his ball close enough to
get down in one putt. He did play a great stroke,
but he was fifteen feet from the hole in three and
his opponent had played only two.

Just what Brownlow was thinking of when he hit
his approach putt will not be known unless the
young man himself offers an explanation. From a
touch that was almost silky, he suddenly hit a
nervous crude coarse putt and his ball rolled far
beyond, so far, in fact, that he was called upon to
putt again. He did manage to slide this one close,
but he had passed up a golden opportunity. Jesse
was unequal to the task of holing the fifteen-footer,

and on they went to the twentieth. Brownlow was down the middle. Sweetser was in the rough to the right and had to play over a pot trap on the corner of the green. His shot was successful, but it stopped on the hard green almost immediately and was a long way from home.

His opponent, with a simple little pitch-and-run shot with nothing in the way, played a sloppy approach, and his ball only just did reach the green. That particular green was the fastest one at Muirfield and Brownlow must have borne this in mind when he putted, because he was ten feet short. Sweetser figured the mist that had been collecting in the twilight had probably slowed down the speed of the green, putted too boldly, and ran twelve feet over. Both players were on edge, and with them the huge gallery that watched every shot. Sweetser had not holed a single putt all day long, and those of us who wanted him to win thought he must have one putt in that old putter of his. He caused a thrill of joy by holing out, which put the issue squarely up to Mr. Brownlow. This young man was by no manner of means through with his deadly work, and he plunked as neat a putt as you ever saw smack into the cup. It was nerve-racking, and something had to give.

Brownlow had the honor. He had driven beautifully, and no one expected him to fall down on his tee shot. The third hole called for a drive and a

long pitch, and there was no great problem to the
tee shot. The strain was beginning to tell, and
while the spirit was willing the flesh proved weak.
Out of a clear sky Brownlow came down on top of
his ball and it rolled a mere fifty yards or so off the
tee precluding any possibility of the player getting
home in the required number of strokes. Sweetser
had pulled himself together and lashed a great drive
far down the fairway. That settled the match beyond further doubt, and it was a tired though
happy American who hurried himself off to bed for
the final match the next day. That contest between
Brownlow and Sweetser was the most dramatic
golf match that has ever been played, in my opinion, and I have never witnessed a greater exhibition of courage and skill than that shown by both
players.

The final between Archie Simpson and Sweetser
was an anti-climax. The American won going
away, and after a few holes had been played, it was
apparent that Sweetser was the better player.
Simpson killed whatever chances he might have
had by driving at breakneck speed to the course to
keep his appointment, and he never did get his
nerves in shape for the match. It is a good thing
for golfers to give themselves plenty of time by
arriving at the scene beforehand and thus enable
jumpy nerves to quiet themselves before the competition.

CHAPTER XI

BOBBY JONES — AND OTHERS — BEAT ME

NINETEEN-TWENTY-SIX was a memorable golfing year. The open championship was played at Scioto, Columbus, Ohio, and the brilliant young professional Joe Turnesa had the title wrapped up, with seven holes left to be played. Overanxiety ruined him and gave Bobby Jones an opportunity which he accepted in great shape. Where Turnesa collapsed, Jones made up the lost ground, and he came to the final hole needing a four to win. The hole was par five and measured approximately four hundred and eighty yards. Scioto fairways were very narrow and carved through long grass that resembled wheat-fields. I can still see Watts Gunn searching for his ball with the grass almost up to his waist, and saying he hoped he did not find it, because his score was terrible, and he wanted some good reason for not turning in his card.

Anyway, there was Bobby on that last tee gazing down the narrow, winding fairway. He hit a perfectly colossal tee shot that followed the outline of the rough and then, with just the right amount of bend, it scampered along, finally resting in the geographical middle three hundred and twenty yards from where it started. The fact that his mashie iron nearly hit the pin and stopped ten feet from the cup seemed nothing as compared to that drive. Every spectator who followed knew he would hit the green with his second after such a tee shot, and the four that followed was merely routine.

One of the features of the amateur championship played that year at Baltusrol was the qualifying round. Seven players were tied for six places and I was one of the hapless seven. It was the second successive time, and I can only say that I wish each and every one of those spectators who watched the cards returned at the eighteenth green and wished for a big play-off would get into one themselves sometime, and then perhaps they would realize what a sorry experience it is.

Well, there we were. Frank Dyer topped his drive. Eddie Held hooked his, and a fence was the only thing that saved it from going out of bounds, the penalty for such a mistake meaning loss of stroke and distance. Someone else or maybe two golfers, sliced into trouble. Then I was called to the tee. I shut my eyes, swung, and saw my ball sailing down the fairway, and I thought my troubles were over. The hole was four hundred and ninety yards long, and it was a foregone conclusion that a five would qualify. From where my ball lay, I could reach the green with a number two iron.

There was no point in playing for the green because one might get caught up in the trap on the left. Therefore, when it was my shot, I was going to show my partners in crime a fine piece of judgment by deliberately hitting well to the right. My intentions were good, but my execution was horrible. Instead of playing to the right, I hit the ball on the toe of my iron and saw it pull badly to the spot I had been trying to avoid. It seemed as though millions followed us toward the green. I had hoped my ball might have escaped the pit, but then I had no fear of playing from the trap because it was near the green, and I like to play explosive shots from the sand. When I reached my ball, I discovered it had barely rolled over the edge of the fairway into an overhanging lie, half in the trap and half out. Fownes was refereeing the play-off, and I inwardly wished he would not see me. Bill did nothing of the sort. He carefully measured at the glance of an eye the distances of the various balls and then ordered me to play. Back of the green was a throng of people and beyond them was the inevitable out-of-bounds. When the crowd moved away from the back of the green, my heart came up in my mouth because the only avenue of escape was removed, that of crashing the ball into the crowd and having it stop. Bill stood at the pin. I had a big niblick. I took a swing at the fairway in back of my ball for all I was worth, felt the ball meet the face of the club, saw a huge divot fly through the air, and then the ball. It had been hammered out of the desperate lie through sheer power, and what was even better came to rest one foot, twelve inches from the cup. Bill asked me if I wished to putt out. I did, holed a four, and without waiting for the rest to play, I walked back to the clubhouse with the full knowledge that I had succeeded in qualifying.

In the second round against Eustace Storey, an English chap, I ran wild on the putting greens. On the second green I dropped an eight-foot putt. On the third, a twenty-footer. On the fourth, a thirty-footer. On the fifth one, at least forty feet. My second to the sixth green was trapped, but an explosive shot left me a fifteen-foot putt, and that was dropped. Five successive greens I had taken but one putt. Walking to the seventh tee, Eustace, who is one of the greatest sportsmen in the world, looked me square in the eye and said, 'I have a good mind to wrap this putter of mine around your neck.' I should not have blamed him at all.

I fell away from this putting streak for a few holes, but on the eleventh, one of thirty-five feet dropped. One might think I must have smothered Storey, but it was just as well for me I had putted so phenomenally because I was hard-pressed to beat him by two and one. A friend of mine was sitting behind the fourth green watching the players as they came along. My pitch had only just carried the pond and the ball was thirty feet from the cup. My friend offered to wager one against twenty I would hole my putt. A friend of his accepted and lost twenty dollars. We came to the fifth green. 'What are the odds against Francis holing this putt?' said my friend. 'Forty to one,' said the other. My friend took the short end, and this time collected forty dollars more from his cousin. That ended the betting between the two.

In the first round George Von Elm played Ellsworth Augustus, a strapping lad from Cleveland. Von Elm had to play the last two holes in better than par to keep the match even. It was an eighteen-hole match. Playing the extra hole, Von Elm was trapped with his second and Augustus was on the green. Von Elm blasted out, took two putts, and won the hole when his opponent required four putts. Von Elm beat Bobby Jones in the finals, and I say this now to show how a little thing can change the entire aspects of a championship. Von Elm could have been beaten in the first round, and yet he went on to win the championship.

I bumped into Bobby Jones in the semi-finals. Bobby won the first hole with a four. We both got on the second green in two, and I had to putt first from twenty feet. Bobby was fifteen feet away. I putted and played my ball on the very edge of the cup. A large gallery was following. Bobby walked forward to see how much leeway he could take with his putt without disturbing my ball, which happened to be on the opposite side of the hole. And then he did not wish to stymie himself. He examined my ball carefully, looked at me and smiled, and then turned and started to walk back to his own ball. As he did so, the crowd broke out in laughter. I could not understand it. Neither could Bobby. He was studying his line of putt, and then stopped suddenly. 'Where is your ball?' I looked around, and could not see it. While Bobby's back was turned, my ball had dropped in, and that was the cause of the gallery's mirth.

That piece of luck squared the match, and we halved every one of the next twelve holes in fine golf. Bobby put on the pressure from then on and we retired for luncheon with me three down. I knocked a full spoon shot a foot from the first hole in the afternoon, and the three, two under par, gave me a win. Par on the nine outgoing holes was 37, and I played them in 34. Against the ordinary human this would reduce any deficiency of holes, but Mr. Jones waltzed out in 33, and I turned four down. The match ended five up and four to play in favor of Bobby, and to give you some idea of what I was up against, I had par on the last four holes for a 69, and was outclassed.

That same fall a match was arranged between Walter Hagen and myself at the Sandy Burr

Country Club, Wayland, Massachusetts. It was to be a thirty-six-hole contest, eighteen one afternoon and eighteen the following day. The first day the match was close, with Hagen leading by a hole playing the eighteenth. The last green was new and consequently very rough, and after getting home in two, I took three putts. Hagen was also on in two. He putted and fell far short. His next slipped a foot by. Hagen then grasped his putter very short and, hastily hitting his ball, missed. He explained to the referee Everett Litchfield that he thought I had conceded him the putt until he noticed me standing by with arms folded. Then he realized I intended that he should putt his ball. He had taken a short grip on the putter and carelessly tapped his ball.

In the locker room I suggested that Hagen be given a five, but he would not have it, showing his sportsmanship by saying I had not given him that putt, and therefore it was not fair to concede it after he had missed. The final day everything went right for me. I played the first nine holes in 32, made up of five threes, four of which came successively, three fours, and a five. This spurt gave me a six-hole lead, and I won by seven up and five to play. I never relinquished the driving honor until the seventeenth tee. This match did not mean a thing, apart from the satisfaction of beating a man of the caliber of Walter Hagen. However, the experience was worth while, because one can gain a lot, competitively speaking, in such contests.

As an example of what I mean, let us take Hagen's play on the sixth hole. Hagen had played over the green to a trap in a miserable spot. My second was nicely on, about twelve feet from the cup. I was three up at the time, and Hagen could ill-afford to lose that hole. His ball was on the back edge of the trap with a downhill lie. It was out of the question to explode his ball from the sand, because there was no sand behind it. Moreover, the green sloped abruptly away from him and there was little opportunity to hold the ball near the cup on an explosive shot. With such a hopeless outlook, Hagen, who has been referred to by George Duncan as a golfing freak, attempted a shot that none but he would think of. He examined the side of the trap far to the right of what seemed to be the proper line, selected a straight-faced iron, and punched his ball into the banking. It kicked sharply to the left and barely failed by the merest fraction of an inch to reach the edge of the green. Another turn of that ball would have taken it onto the pulling surface and it would then have rolled stone dead. It was the only chance he had of getting close enough for the four, and that his gamble missed does not, in my opinion, spoil the shot in any way, for it was the effort of the master.

The Minikahda Club, at Minneapolis, Minnesota, was the scene of the 1927 national amateur championship, and no course could have been in finer condition than this one. Irrigated fairways freshened the turf and the greens were perfect in texture. The committee in charge of the affair went to unlimited trouble in making the event one to be remembered. They laboriously examined weather conditions for a period of fifteen years and discovered that on the average the temperature was more pleasant and cool the third week in August than at any other time of the golfing season. The result was the tournament dates were established from August 22 through the 27th, and there was hardly a day when a light sweater was not a comfortable garment to wear.

The first eighteen-hole qualifying round brought two young players to the fore, the steady and consistent Gene Homans and the brilliant and far-driving Phillips Finlay. In the end it was Bobby Jones who supplied the fireworks, for with a brilliant round of 67 or 68 he won the qualifying round. A most unusual thing happened to George Voigt and no doubt had much to do with his failure to qualify. Playing the short sixth hole, one hundred and seventy yards in length, Voigt put his iron shot eight feet from the cup. His qualifying partner followed suit with another great shot, and, as his ball rolled toward the hole, according to spectators near the green, it struck Voigt's

183

and moved it slightly. Voigt and his partner could not see the performance from the tee. Reaching the green, Voigt was informed what had taken place. The rules for such a happening in medal competition specifically state that the ball must be replaced as near as possible to where it originally was, under penalty of disqualification. Voigt did not know what to do. He decided to putt the ball from where it was and then drop a provisional ball and putt that one from where the spectators thought it was. He missed the putt for the two with the first and dropped the putt with the second ball. Voigt was completely upset by the incident and did not know whether he had disqualified himself or not. In this confused state of mind, his play slipped badly and he failed to qualify.

Bobby Jones found himself in a very tough spot in his first-round match. Opposed to Maurice McCarthy, a quiet, black-haired youngster from New York, he was in grave danger of elimination. Five holes from home, Bobby was two down. Then McCarthy missed a wee putt for a half and Jones turned on the steam to win by two holes. This was the highlight of that first round. The champion George Von Elm got through the first round without trouble, but he found plenty of difficulty with Harry Legg of Minikahda in the second. Legg had won the trans-Mississippi championship at least seven times, and any man with such a record must know something about the game of golf. He knew enough about the great game to stick with Von Elm all the way, and finally put him out of the running on the home hole.

I had beaten Billy Sixty of Milwaukee six up and five to play in the opening round, and my old rival Max Marston in the next, and so had reached the third round. My opponent was Phillips Finlay. In years gone by I had played at some time or other with Abe Mitchell, Ted Ray, and Jesse Guilford, so I had some idea of long hitting, but I never saw anything to beat the driving of Finlay for sheer distance. He was so far beyond me on every tee shot that I could hardly see his ball. However, matches are not won from the tee, and that was my salvation. I was getting sufficient length myself to reach greens in two, and once in a while an errant tee shot permitted me to cash in.

At the end of the morning round I was two holes to the good. I drove a fine tee shot down the middle of the fairway after luncheon, and when Finlay hooked his behind a tall spruce tree, I rightfully expected to become three up. His ball was but a few feet from the trunk of the tree and there seemed no possible way of getting around it. Finlay reviewed the situation with care, chose a niblick, opened up the face to the point where the back of the niblick was almost flat on the ground, and then

185

proceeded to hit for all he was worth. The ball rose almost perpendicularly, cleared the tree and the trap guarding the green, and stopped a foot from the hole. Needless to say, he won the hole. Now only one up, I sliced my drive out of bounds on the second, after Finlay had driven a beauty. There were so many possible opportunities to hit out of bounds, the United States Golf Association decided the penalty would be distance only. Therefore, I was permitted to tee another. This was hit accurately enough, and left me a three iron to the four-hundred-and-forty-yard hole. I was still away and playing three. Finlay had played one. I was fighting to hang onto the thin lead, because he was no fellow to monkey with, and we should soon be coming to long holes. With a three iron I smashed the ball for all I was worth and saw it traveling on a line for the hole. It hit four feet from the cup and stopped dead two feet away. That shot saved the hole and won the match, because thereafter I settled down and gave Finlay no more such opportunities.

Bobby Jones was just beginning to hit his best match-play form, and eliminated Harrison Johnston, whom everybody calls 'Jimmy,' by ten up and nine to play. Chick Evans and Roland McKenzie were the other semi-finalists. This pair had a great match that was not settled until thirty-seven holes had been played, with Evans the winner. Once again I found myself against Robert Tyre Jones, Jr., in a semi-final match, and those of you who think Bobby is a bargain in a semi-final match should take him on sometime. My memory is a bit hazy, but I believe the first four holes were halved in par figures. From then on it was just a procession. Bobby was positively ruthless. You just cannot play your game. If you play well, he will go you one better. He gives you no openings whatsoever, and you have to make your own bed. I made mine and was put to sleep by another margin of eleven down and ten to play.

I can only describe a match against Bobby in this manner: It is just as though you got your hand caught in a buzz saw. He coasts along serenely waiting for you to miss a shot, and the moment you do, he has you on the hook and you never get off. If the young man were human, he would make a mistake once in a while, but he never makes any mistakes. He manages to do everything better than anybody else. He can drive straighter than any man living. He is perfectly machinelike in his iron play, and on the greens he is a demon. If you can beat that type of man, I should like the recipe. But he is more than a great golfer. He is a grand competitor.

Chick Evans was against the same thing in the finals. Evans did not play poorly by any manner of means. Yet, like many of the others, he was

blasted out of the lot by a barrage of threes and
fours, and if one were to analyze Chick's golf the
day Bobby beat him eight and seven for the
amateur title of 1927, one would be forced to admit
that Evans played great golf. And still he was
outclassed.

As an instance of the heights Bobby can scale
when he wishes to do so, let me tell you about
the ninth hole at Minikahda. This hole measures
five hundred and sixty yards in length and is the
longest hole on the course. The tee shot has to be
played slightly to the left to avoid the out-of-
bounds stakes on the right. The last two hundred
and fifty yards are up a steep grade, and if ever
a hole was a three-shotter, it is this one. Before
the championship one of the members of the club
made a substantial wager at very inviting odds that
a three would not be made on the hole during the
championship. There were many fours made —
I had one myself; but to get a three, the player
had to hole a sizable approach. Now and again a
second shot would come fairly close to the green,
but owing to the incline, it was generally felt the
green was beyond the range of any living human
in two shots. Then came the last time Bobby was
to play it. He threw caution to the winds and
cracked a long tee shot down the right-hand side
of the fairway, and saved himself many yards by
doing so. Then out came his ivory-faced spoon, a

club that George Duncan had given him. He hit his ball with power and it climbed into the air. It kept on climbing. It landed on the green. It not only landed on the green, but a foot from the cup! And it stayed there. Yes. He made that hole in three, and the member lost his bet.

CHAPTER XII

MR. JONES PLAYS MR. GORTON
AT BRAE–BURN

IN 1928, it was the turn for the Britons to send a Walker Cup team to this country to play for the Walker Cup, and the Chicago Golf Club, at Wheaton, Illinois, was the course chosen. I had not seen this layout since 1912, and my recollection of the Chicago Golf Club, previous to my visit in 1928, was of an old-fashioned test, with cross-bunkers instead of the modern idea of trapping. On almost every hole there was a huge bunker, placed for a missed tee shot or a half-hit second. This was the sort of test I had pictured, though, to be sure, I knew the Chicago Golf Club had brought its course up to the times. As I stood on the first tee and gazed toward the hole, it looked quite the same with the exception of a few traps near the green. The cross-bunker had been removed on the second hole, and it was entirely different. As I played over the course, it impressed me as one of the fine ones of the country, and so it was.

A great feeling of friendliness exists between the members of the Walker Cup teams, and it is customary in practice rounds to indulge in fourball matches, an American and a Briton playing against an American and a Briton. In one of these practice sessions I was opposed to Bobby Jones, with Phil Perkins as a partner. For some reason or other I seemed to be putting well — that is to say, I was stroking my ball nicely on the greens — but for the life of me I could not drop a putt. On the other hand, Bobby Jones appeared to me to be putting carelessly, and yet he was popping them into the hole from all distances. I complained to Bobby about my putting and asked him to criticize my efforts. Bob watched me for a few holes and said, 'You are trying too hard to hole your putts. Hit your ball in the general direction of the hole and see what happens.' I tried this. All of a sudden the putts began dropping in. The carefree attitude furnished just the proper amount of relaxation, and from that day on I had no further trouble on the greens.

Two days before the Walker Cup matches, a medal-play tournament was held at Flossmoor, as a memorial to Warren K. Wood, one of the best of the Mid-Western golfers who had passed on to his reward. Flossmoor was his home course, so out of respect to his memory the eight British and eight American Walker Cup players entered the event. Fourball matches were arranged, and in one of these Watts Gunn and Major Hezlet of England played with John Beck, also an Englishman, and myself. The first tee was crowded with spectators waiting for the match in which Bobby Jones was to play. Our four were placed just ahead.

Major Hezlet is an imposing person, husky and tall, and his spread-eagle stance attracts everyone. The Major stepped onto the tee, smashed a terrific drive straight down the fairway, and the crowd applauded generously. Watts Gunn followed suit amidst another outburst. I followed, and the tee shot was also well received, and the three balls down the fairway two hundred and fifty yards away could have been covered by a blanket. Then John Beck took the tee. He half-topped his tee shot, and it rolled along the ground down the middle, but not very far. John Beck is one of the most delightful fellows imaginable, a splendid golfer and a humorist. He was somewhat embarrassed at his failure to drive out where our balls lay, and his embarrassment was accentuated by the fact that two or three of the spectators applauded good-naturedly. As we walked down the fairway, Beck, chuckling to himself, broke into laughter, and said, 'I received a mild round of applause for direction, only.' We all had a laugh over that.

There were many fine players in the field, not merely those playing on the Walker Cup teams. Flossmoor was stretched to the limit which made the play long as well as difficult, and when Johnny Dawson streaked his way over the eighteen holes in 71, it was generally conceded that he would turn out to be the winner. Dawson, a wonderful golfer, was not on our Walker Cup team, and his round was a beauty from the point of view of brilliancy and consistency. Several members of the American Walker Cup team played well, but none could touch Dawson's 71. When Bobby Jones cruised out in a spotty sort of 37, none thought he had a chance. Then he ran wild completely. He started in as follows, 3–3–4–3–3–3–3, for the first seven holes on the last nine. This burst was five under par. The seventeenth and eighteenth holes at Flossmoor are mighty hard. Par is five, and while par is not particularly hard to do, they are the kind of holes where the golfer goes searching for fours and finds sixes instead. Bobby made his four on the seventeenth. A drive and wonderful brassie put him on the long eighteenth in two and he had a thirty-foot putt left for a three and a nine-hole score of 29. He failed by a cat's whisker to sink the long putt, but the thirty gave him a score of 67, too wonderful to describe. Of course this won for him the Wood Memorial Cup.

We returned to the Chicago Golf Club to have one more whack at the course the day before the Walker Cup foursomes. Bobby and I were rooming together. The night before the match, we discussed foursome play. British players indulge in this type of play frequently, and they are more at home in foursome competition than our own boys who seldom play anything but single or fourball games. Therefore, we had a sort of fight talk and agreed if we were to get off to a good start we must give nothing away to begin with. With this idea in mind, the American boys left the tee on edge, prepared to whip themselves into a nice lead on the early holes. That is just what did not happen.

At the end of five holes, each of the American teams was down to its British opponent. 'Jimmy' Johnston and I were three down to Tony Torrance and Eustace Storey. Watts Gunn and Roland McKenzie, all over the lot, were four down. However, we all steadied in the nick of time, with the result that the Americans won every match in spite of the slow start. Eight singles were the order for the second day. Bobby Jones proved a great leader and smothered Phil Perkins, British amateur champion, thirteen down and twelve to play. The first seven matches came our way. Chick Evans was having a fine match with Tony Torrance and came to the last hole square. Evans was just short of the green in two and Torrance in the like was over. Torrance chipped back stone dead and his four gave him a win and the only British victory.

From Chicago, the two teams repaired East, to Brae-Burn, for the amateur championship. Brae-Burn is in West Newton, Massachusetts, a long, exacting course, well-trapped, with splendid fairways and putting greens. It is a course that can

194

be scored over satisfactorily, but one that will give nothing away. The scoring was excellent, lower than I expected, and four or five men tied at 157 for the top score. George Voigt won the medal with a thirty-six-hole total of 143, which was great golf. Medal rounds, particularly those that form part of the amateur championship, are nerve-racking affairs. Competition has become so keen that any one of fifty golfers is fully able to qualify, if he plays his normal game. I doubt if anybody in the tournament knew the Brae-Burn course more thoroughly than I did, and yet I had all sorts of trouble.

After playing a fair round the first day and scoring a 78, everything went wrong the second day. Standing on the eighth tee, I had par for the next two holes for an outward round of 42. I could do nothing correctly. When I hit a decent tee shot, I would spoil this with a wretched iron. If I combined a fine tee shot with an equally satisfactory iron, three putts followed. Therefore, in my frame of mind the par figures of 3–4 seemed most unlikely.

The eighth hole called for a long spoon shot or brassie to a well-trapped green. I hit my ball to the left to take advantage of the roll. But I hit it too far to the left and caught the trap. Fortunately, although in the trap, my ball was not far from the hole, and I can sometimes get an explosion shot near the pin on such occasions. My ball was well buried in a deep footprint, and I was desperate. I shut my eyes after taking a mighty swing at the ball, and to my great joy it came out of the trap perfectly and then rolled easily toward the hole, finally stopping an inch or two away. I got the three.

I pulled my tee shot to the rough at the ninth, but luck was with me and I pitched the ball three feet from the cup and got another three. Forty-one to the turn left me a small chance, provided I could play the last nine holes in good style. I might say the last nine at Brae-Burn are several strokes harder than the first.

I had a putt for an eagle three on the long tenth, but the four I made was very welcome. The eleventh is a par four, but par is rather generous. I dropped a long putt for three. This was a good start. The short twelfth was made in three, and I picked up another stroke on the long thirteenth by picking up a four. A par five came on the fourteenth.

After an excellent drive to the fifteenth, I half-topped my pitch and lost a stroke to par. However, in spite of the error I was sailing along in good shape, and unless something happened on the last three holes, I was safely in. The four on the sixteenth was useful. Then came the long one-shot seventeenth. A search for a three usually brings a five or six. I was even fours to that point, and could ill-afford to take unnecessary risks. Therefore a safe four placed me on the last tee with a par four for a 77.

The tee on the eighteenth had been placed far back, and it took a tremendous drive to carry the brook. On both sides of the fairway were woods, and a wild shot, or one that did not carry the brook, meant sudden and complete disaster. I do not believe I have ever hit a ball so hard as I hit that last tee shot. And I hit it right on the nose. I could feel it all the way up and through the shaft. It not only landed on the fairway, but had a great roll. It gave me a mashie shot for the green. I made no mistake and put that ball on the green a dozen feet from the hole. The green was fast, and, after taking a quick glance, I putted carefully so as not to overrun the hole by too big a margin, and when that ball dropped out of sight for a three, I was the most elated person in the world. I was home in 35, around in 76, and qualified very safely. It was a battle, one of the toughest I have ever had, and I believe it killed whatever chances I might have had to go a few rounds in match play.

The next morning I drew Phillips Finlay. Through no particular fault of my own, I was four up at the eighth. I had the better of two shots to the ninth green, but Finlay, who had been playing atrociously, staggered me for a second by holing out from the edge of the green. Then he started to play the kind of golf he can play and I just as quickly proceeded to pass him hole after hole. At the sixteenth we were even. Finlay smashed a terrific iron, into the wind ten feet from the hole at the seventeenth, and won. He also won the last one and the match, and I was through.

That 1928 championship was just one more procession for Bobby Jones. Once he got through the eighteen-hole match-play rounds, there was no one in his class. But easily the feature of that event was Jones's match with Ray Gorton in the second round, and it must go down in his memory as one of the hardest he has ever had. Gorton is what I call a week-end golfer; that is to say, he seldom participates in competition and his only golf is played Saturday afternoons and Sunday mornings. Nevertheless, he is a great player and a wonderful sportsman. A round of golf, whether or not it is in the national amateur championship, is just another round to him. Further, the fact that he plays so little means nothing, because he can always take care of himself, especially at Brae-Burn, his home course.

Neither Jones nor Gorton played the first nine holes well, at which point in the match Gorton was leading by a hole. There was enough good golf to make the game interesting. The gallery was thrilled to think Gorton was making a match, and when both players hit two great brassie seconds to the four-hundred-and-ninety-yard hole, the excitement was tremendous. Bobby had to putt first and touched the cup for a three, the ball stopping inches away. Then Ray bravely dropped his putt for a winning three and became two up.

The eleventh was played brilliantly. Gorton's second, played with an iron, left him thirty feet from the hole. Bobby was a few feet closer. Ray hit his putt smoothly and it rolled as true as a die into the hole. That placed the issue squarely up to Mr. Jones. He could not afford to lose that one, because that would give his opponent a three-hole lead, and no one can spot Ray Gorton three holes with seven to play and hope to beat him. Jones, I believe, has a seventh sense in golf. He always knows what to do, and what is more, he knows when to do it. Into the hole went his putt for a halving three.

On the next green Gorton wavered for a second, took three putts, and lost a mighty valuable hole, and the wise boys said, 'Here is the beginning of the end.' Nothing of the kind happened. Two good halves followed, and Bobby finally evened the match on the fifteenth by pitching stone dead. The sixteenth brought another half. Then that tough seventeenth provided a few more thrills, for both failed to reach the green from the tee. Gorton's approach rolled close to the hole. Bobby chipped too boldly and ran ten feet beyond. I remember standing on the hillside directly in back of the green and seeing that Bobby had an ugly putt, downhill. It was a misty afternoon and the green was covered with dew. Ordinarily this in itself is bothersome, because it is hard to tell just how to hit the ball. Some greens are less affected than others in so far as the speed is concerned. Bobby had to borrow several inches to the left, after which another roll had to be accounted for. A failure meant the match. Bobby tapped the ball and it dropped. Then came the eighteenth. Jones led off by pushing a long tee shot off line and dangerously close to a clump of bushes which shut off any possibility of an iron to the green. A straight tee shot might end the match as far as Gorton was concerned. After hitting every previous tee shot as beautifully as possible, Ray made a hopeless mess of his drive. He hit far under it into the mushy turf, and the ball popped up in the air, curled to the left, and settled in the blueberry bushes. He could not play toward the hole. His only avenue of escape from the woods was a recovery to a temporary tee. This merely seemed to delay proceedings, because it definitely meant that Ray must need four shots to reach the green, and assuming he did nothing remarkable, a losing six must result. He reached the tee on his second, banged a long iron up the fairway, and left the gate wide open for Bobby to finish the match. Jones plugged his ball back to the fairway and sent his third plump onto the middle of the green. That appeared to settle the match. Gorton played a splendid fourth, that left him a fifteen-foot sidehill putt for a five. Golfers were not holing fifteen-foot putts on that last green, and it was too much to expect Gorton to hole that one. Bobby had been struggling all the day and chose to play conservatively. Therefore, his approach putt was nursed delicately by the holeside — so delicately that it practically shut out Ray from any possibility of keeping the match alive. He took one of those quick glances at Bobby, a smile crept over his face, and he tackled the job of holing the putt. I can see Ray this minute taking his stance and hitting the ball. It was one of those dying gasps. The ball was hit firmly and it rolled straight for the other. Then it began to lose its power, and as it did, it slid by Jones's ball and popped out of sight for as fine a five as I have ever seen on any golf course. The match was square.

In the misty, smoky, waning daylight, the two moved on to the nineteenth as the gallery rushed helter-skelter for the green. Jones was down the middle with his drive and Gorton deep in the woods. He could only play his ball back to the fairway and waste a shot. Jones pitched to the green, and at last had the game in hand. Gorton hit a third that left him on the green, but a long, long way from the cup. Again I stationed myself in back of the line of putt. Ray hit his ball solidly, and it looked as good as gold as it cut its way through the dew-covered putting surface. As it got close to the hole, it seemed to lose speed and this alone kept it from dropping. It just missed the edge, and at last Ray Gorton was beaten, but what a fight he had put up! If he does nothing else in golfing competition, he can look back on that game because it was one of the finest an amateur has ever put up against the golfing marvel of all time.

From then on it was a romp for Bobby. In the finals his opponent was the British amateur champion, T. Philip Perkins. It is a peculiar thing in golf, but the player who is hitting his ball best seems to get all the fortunate breaks. Perhaps it is a reward for his good golf. On the seventh hole in the afternoon, Bobby was eight up. He hooked his drive badly. The spectators were walking along down the left-hand side of the fairway, when Bobby's ball, heading for the rough and trees, crashed a spectator on the head and rebounded to the middle of the fairway. The unlucky individual, I am told, was carried to the hospital as Mr. Jones was smacking a majestic iron shot eight feet from the pin.

CHAPTER XIII

PLAYING GOLF WITH THE PACIFIC OCEAN

EVERYONE looked forward to the championship of 1929 because Pebble Beach at Del Monte, California, was the spot chosen for the tournament. In February of that winter, as I was walking to my office, I inadvertently put my foot on a piece of ice and landed with a bang. The accident landed me in a hospital for three weeks. The golf season was coming along and I wanted to play in the championship. My doctor told me I could not play for six months. That meant I could not go to Pebble Beach, and you can imagine how I felt. I argued with the doctor, but he was adamant.

Finally, July first came along and I had made several trips to the surgeon's office. He knew I wanted to go to California, and, aside from handling a club now and then at home, I had not hit a ball. About the middle of the month the good doctor asked me if I would like to play golf. I told him I would. 'Then you'd better get in some practice,' was his admonition. Therefore, I got out quietly in the evening, seemed to have no ill effects, and got myself ready for the trip to the coast. And what a trip!

Eugene Clapp of the Tedesco Country Club, Jim

A GAME OF GOLF

Fellowes from Manchester, New Hampshire, Charlie Cross and Henry Lapham of the Unicorn Country Club, Leonard Shearer from the Country Club, Jim Hollis of Woodland, and I had the best trip I have ever had anywhere. The Czar, Charlie Cross, saw to it that everyone was in bed at a seasonable hour each night and up early in the morning, and the affairs of the nation were freely discussed and settled at each sitting.

Pebble Beach is a beautiful place and a grand golf course. The Californians did everything within their power to make visitors comfortable and happy and the weather was something to dream about. The course was as near perfect as it is possible to have one, and with hardly an exception every player of prominence, not only in this country, but abroad, attended. In the qualifying round, Cyril Tolley came to within a hundred yards of the home green with a fine score behind him. Directly in front of him was a high pine. Tolley tried to pitch his ball over the tree. He played a fine shot, but it lacked the necessary altitude, and as it came down, it landed in the topmost part of the seventy-five-foot pine, and stuck there. You could see that ball, firmly lodged in the branch, and Cyril looked up ruefully at it. There was nothing for him to do but go back and play another ball, and this time he did not try to clear the tree. That mishap cost him a seven, but he had several strokes to spare, so it was not so serious as it might have been. After the players had finished their round and the course was closed for the day, a caddie climbed the tree, got the ball, and sold it for fifty dollars.

Eugene Homans and Bobby Jones tied for the low medal round and the match play was on. The defender, Bobby Jones, was drawn against Johnny Goodman, a young lad from Omaha, who had done well in the open championship. Of course Jones carried the gallery, who were seeing the star Atlantan for the first time on the Pacific Coast. Word came back that Bobby had lost the first three holes. It could not be! Then we heard that he was still three down at the eighth. At the end of the tenth, he was only one down. On the eleventh, he holed a thirty-foot putt for a better than par three, and the feeling ran through the gallery that Bobby was off at last. Goodman holed his putt, which was almost as long. Bobby did manage to square the match a hole or two later, but the gamester from Omaha, as cool as could be, hung on like a leech. Playing the last hole, he was one up. Both on in three, Goodman overran his approach putt by four feet and then tapped it in for a half in five that gave him the match. There was plenty of talent left, but it was a keen disappointment to the Californians to have Jones knocked out in the first round. Lawson Little defeated Goodman in the afternoon in a great match. With the tourna-

ment wide open now, we all got busy to see how far
we might go with the favorite removed.

In round three my opponent was Lawson Little,
an eighteen-year-old lad from San Francisco, who
was born in Rhode Island, had lived in various
sections of the country as well as United States
possessions elsewhere, the son of a Colonel in the
United States Army, and a splendid sportsman.
After a few holes had been played, I was not only
impressed with the long hitting of the boy, but the
courage with which he went about playing. Perhaps I spent too much time looking the boy over
because he was winning the holes as I gazed
around. When I finally did settle down to go after
the match, I was three down. To save my life
I could not catch up with him.

At the end of the morning I was down and not
feeling confident. I began to play well, but Little
was hanging on. With four holes to be played, we
were even. I reached the fifteenth green with a
drive and an iron. Little was in the rough to the
right with his second and over the green in an impossible place in three. At last I thought here is
where I establish a winning lead. Little pulled out
a niblick, smashed into his ball, lifted it in the air,
and it hit the downhill portion of the green. It
must go well over. Then, as though the boy had
a string attached to the ball, it stopped suddenly
a quarter of an inch from the cup and I had to do

some extremely careful putting to hole in two, which gave me the win I wanted. What an escape!

The sixteenth was halved. Then we came to the grand one-shot seventeenth with the Pacific lashing away at the rocks in back. The wind was across, and I hit a brassie shot twelve feet from the cup. I was quite pleased with the result because it was a tough hole. Lawson pulled out an iron and pushed it a bit to the right, but made the green. He was a long way from the hole and between his ball and the cup was a shallow trap that cut into the green. He took his putter, putted through the trap, the ball took the roll, and stopped two feet away. I missed my putt, and the hole was halved.

One up and one to play after a trying day, I took plenty of time figuring out where I wanted my drive to go. The Pacific was roaring away on the left, and I did not want to pull a tee shot into the ocean. I saw a sand trap far to the right, and beyond the trap was the rough! The hole was a par five, and no one could reach the green in two. I knew the rough had been well trampled by the gallery, so I proceeded to hit for the trap, feeling that a good tee shot would clear it safely. From the rough I should have a fine lie, and could then approach the green without fear of the water. I never hit a better tee shot in my life, and it felt great. Lawson bit off a goodly portion of the water, as he put everything he had in his drive and his ball, solidly hit, landed in the middle of the fairway.

As I was walking in the general direction of my ball, my caddie, Speck Hammond, said, 'Why did you hit your ball for that trap?'

'Because I did not want to go into the ocean; besides, I shall have a good lie in the rough,' was my reply.

'Do you know how far that trap is?' questioned Speck.

I told him I thought it was two hundred and twenty-five yards.

'That trap is two hundred and fifty yards from the tee and it cannot be carried,' said the caddie. 'Your ball is in the trap.'

I did not believe it, but as we walked along I saw the spectators climb up the bank of the trap and look down into it. Then I knew where my ball was and Speck was just one hundred per cent correct. Lawson was a mile up the middle and it was up to me to reach that green with a third shot. Speck handed me a mashie. I hesitated. The ball was lying beautifully, although near the bank. I could get out safely enough with my mashie, but I could not get home in three with any club in my bag.

'I am going to play a number three iron, Speck; hand me the club.' Speck thought I was out of my head and started to argue. 'Don't argue with me, Speck, I am going to play that number three iron.' I played the club and I can still hear the sand grating the ball as it barely cleared the top of the pit and sailed a hundred and seventy-five yards up the fairway. That put me in range of the green. The wind was against him, but in spite of this, Lawson Little tied a brassie shot onto his drive that was positively colossal. He was forty yards from the green, playing the hole on a line from the tee. With my cross-country method of playing, I was a spoon shot from the green. I never hit a better spoon shot, and my ball cleared the trap guarding the green by a matter of two feet or so. The surface was soft and my ball stopped instantly thirty-five feet from the hole. Then Little went into action. He walked from his ball all the way to the hole, looked the situation over most carefully, and then nearly holed the approach for an eagle three. His ball was just two feet beyond the cup. All I had to do to win the match was to sink that thirty-five footer, and I did, thereby ending as hard a day of golf as I can remember in many a long year. The Colonel, Mrs. Little, and Lawson came to the cottage where I was stopping and we had a delightful visit. I surely did appreciate their thoughtfulness, and experiences of that kind are the things that make golf such a grand old game.

H. Chandler Egan, the champion of 1904, was knocking his opponents over in fine style, and I believe he stopped the aspirations of Von Elm and Sweetser, proving there was still a kick left in an old-timer. My semi-final opponent was Harrison Johnston, and Doctor Willing and Egan were the other two. 'Jimmy' Johnston was too good for me and won rather comfortably by six up and four to play. At one stage of the match between Willing and Egan, the Doctor was no less than eight up. Egan, however, began to whittle down the lead to such an extent that he was finally beaten four and three, which showed his sterling fighting qualities.

Johnston and Willing had a fine match. The turning-point came, I think, on the eighteenth hole in the morning, at which time they were square. Johnston pulled his second shot onto the beach and his ball was lashed up on the sand by the waves, and then pulled back to the water's edge. During one of the recessions of the wave, Johnston stepped forward, hit his ball quickly, and sent it up and over the high wall to the green. That shot won him the hole, and the good Doctor never quite got going thereafter. You know an unexpected recovery is most disconcerting, particularly if it catches you unprepared.

In one of my rounds at Pebble Beach, I was five up and five to play on Clarence Hubby, of Waco, Texas. The fourteenth hole was a good three-shotter, and my third reposed safely on the green fifteen feet from the hole. Hubby was well beyond the green, in the rough, with an ugly shot to play.

The worst I expected was a halved hole, which would give me the match. In order to get the half, Hubby had to play a remarkable stroke. That is just what he did. With a straight-faced iron he rolled his ball through the rough, up the bank, to the green, and it forthwith slipped into the cup for a winning four. Fortunately, I ended the match on the next hole, but I have often wondered how I should have felt if that same thing had happened when we were even and playing the last hole of the match.

CHAPTER XIV

THE GREAT JONES YEAR

Now we come to the year 1930, which in many ways was the most remarkable golfing season I can remember. A team of American amateurs went abroad to play in the British amateur championship and the Walker Cup matches. Bobby Jones was captain, and as team mates he had Von Elm, Johnston, Voigt, McKenzie, Moe, Willing, and myself. It was a good team, with experience and ability as a background. Moe and Voigt were newcomers, but their record justified their selection. Sandwich was the place chosen for the matches, and after a few days of practice around the London courses the team went on to Sandwich. We were quartered at Ramsgate, a popular English watering-place, and the trip was made from Ramsgate to Sandwich by omnibus each day.

Jones showed his unselfishness by placing Jimmy Johnston, our amateur champion, in the number one position opposed to Cyril Tolley. Many thought Bobby should play number one himself, owing to his brilliant record, but in appointing Jim to the honor place, he was only rewarding Johnston and recognizing the amateur champion as a great golfer. That his judgment was correct was borne out when Jimmy beat Cyril Tolley in the lead-off match in the singles. The foursomes came first, and the American team won three of the four contests, which gave them a beautiful start toward the retention of the Walker Cup. The two Vs, Voigt and Von Elm, were the only losers, falling before Tolley and Wethered, a great foursomes pair.

My partner was Jimmy Johnston, and we had a hard game against our British opponents because time after time I left my partner in trouble. For some reason or other I could not do anything well on the greens. It was bad enough to miss many short putts, but on apparently simple approach putts I constantly left Johnston well away from the hole and he never missed a single one all day long. For example, we were even with four holes to be played. Our third shot was nicely on the green at the fifteenth in three. The Britons had played four and were a long way from the cup. Two putts would give us a win, and a one-hole lead at that stage was highly important. My ball was thirty feet away. With my putting confidence completely gone, I putted half that distance, and then Johnston stepped up and dropped the putt for a win.

An amusing thing happened during our match. There are two holes at Sandwich, the tee shots of which are identical. They are the seventh and the eleventh. The tees are in a hollow, and the drive must be made over a high piece of ground. After the tee shot there is nothing similar about the holes. The seventh is a long testing four, impossible to reach in two against the wind, whereas the eleventh measures three hundred and eighty yards. It was my turn to drive for our side and Johnston stationed himself on the hill in front of the seventh tee, where he could better see the result of my tee shot. I drove a good one. Jimmy walked ahead and selected an iron for the next. We had an understanding that we would not interfere with one another unless information was solicited. I thought it strange that Johnston should be using an iron when it was obvious the shot called for full wood. Then I decided he had a bad lie. Jim hit a fine iron, but was seventy-five yards short of the green. Our opponents were practically home in two. When I came up to Jimmy there was a look of surprise on his face and I asked him what had happened. He looked at me with a sickly smile on his face and said, 'Francis, I am sorry; I figured I was playing the eleventh hole and used a number three iron when I should have given it the works.' We had a good laugh over the incident, and it was soon forgotten.

The Americans won seven of the eight singles and retained the Cup. I was the only loser. My opponent, Tony Torrance, recently chosen captain of the British team for this year (1932), was altogether too good for me. He was invincible and played splendidly all day long, his morning round of 70 being one of the best, especially the way he got it. He never made a mistake. His lead of five holes was too great a handicap for me the way he was hitting his ball, and he had little to do in finishing me by seven down and six to play. A wonderful match was going on just in back of us, and Tony and I finished just in time to see Don Moe, the American, hole a thirty-foot putt on the twelfth green to square his match with 'Bill' Stout, the Englishman. I could not believe the match was even, because I knew Moe was four down in the morning, and when Stout started 3–3–3, after luncheon, he had run his lead to seven up. Yet here was Moe even up. What had happened? Moe had won seven of the next nine holes. He had gone out in 32. It was remarkable golf on a stiff test. They battled on. The thirteenth was halved. On the fourteenth, a very long and hard par five hole, Moe planted a brassie shot on the green in two and won the hole to take the lead. The fifteenth, another long one, went to Stout.

Both reached the green on the short sixteenth. Stout put his long putt stone dead. Moe was short with his and had to drop an eight-footer for a half. The seventeenth likewise saw the two still even, and they headed for the final hole just where they started in the morning after thirty-five holes of brilliant playing. Stout is a terrific hitter and he hammered a mighty drive down the fairway. Moe followed with one just a few yards behind. The last hole at Sandwich is about four hundred and sixty yards long, and since the wind is invariably against the player, it is very seldom reached in two shots. I had seen Jones and Wethered with two full wooden shots fail to get home.

Moe had to play first, and I was amazed to see him pick out a number two iron. I did not think he had a chance of getting home. He hit that two iron on the nose and the ball actually carried to the green on a dead line for the flag. It hopped in the air and rolled for the pin. It barely missed the marker and stopped three feet from the hole. Never have I seen a more wonderful iron shot in my life, taking into consideration the tenseness of the competition and what it meant. A roar of approval went up from the crowd surrounding the green, a token of real admiration for a fighting American. The British sporting public are excellent sportsmen. They naturally hoped Stout would win, but their feelings were smothered when Moe played his spectacular stroke. Stout pulled his ball to the left of the green, but, unless he placed his ball alongside Donald's, it mattered little. In the morning Stout had got around in 68. That three of Moe's gave him a 67, a stroke under the course record.

The Great Jones Year

In the locker room after the match, the British and American players were changing their shoes. In the group was Bill Stout, and he gazed out of a window, not sadly, but in meditation. Then, during a lull in the conversations that ran through the room, Stout got up, moved over to Don Moe, and said, 'Donald, that was not golf, that was a visitation from God.' And it was not said irreverently or with disappointment.

From Sandwich we bundled up and set forth for St. Andrews, the scene of the British amateur championship. I shall never forget my feelings when I found I was drawn against Joshua Crane in the first round. Crane was an old Bostonian who had taken up a residence in London. He was a great athlete in his day and at one time coached the Harvard football team. He was a champion at court tennis and an outstanding polo player. Just one of those fellows who play all games well. He had never taken golf seriously until his polo days were over, but he knew enough about the game to play it well. What made me so concerned over our match was the fact that we had many friends in common, and I knew if he beat me there would be plenty of explaining to do. I had not been playing well and anything can happen at St. Andrews, so I was fearful of the outcome.

My opponent, however, gave me many opportunities to win holes and I managed to get him out

217

of the way by five up and three. My next ad-
versary was a prominent English soccer player
named Bowers. He played steadily, opened up
a nice lead for himself, and at the ninth I was three
down. I lost the twelfth and was then in the bad
position of being four down and six to play. When
the seventeenth had been played, I had retrieved
three of the four holes and faced the home hole but
one to the bad. The fairway was hard, the wind
behind us, and I hit a tee shot that reached the
front edge of the green three hundred and sixty
yards away. Bowers sliced his drive, and the ball,
landing on the roadway, bounded forward to a
point where it was hole-high with the green, and
behind a fence that was latticed. He had to play,
and I thought here is my chance to square this
match, because he will have to sacrifice a stroke
before getting to the green. There was a small
opening about six inches square and Mr. Bowers
picked the opening very deftly and put his ball on,
fifteen feet from the cup. That was not only
a surprise, but a shock. I do not know how I did it,
but with a putter I rolled my ball to within two
feet of the cup and won the hole. We halved the
nineteenth and also the twentieth. I had the
twenty-first, the third extra, sewed up apparently
beyond all doubt when I put my pitch shot fifteen
feet from the pin. Bowers took three to reach the
green and then placed his fourth dead. All I had to

do was to get down in two putts to end the match. My putting was atrocious, but I did not see how I could possibly take more than two putts from fifteen feet on a perfectly flat putting surface. I knew the green was like a streak of lightning and I did try to putt cautiously, but I had no control whatsoever over the putter and my first putt slipped eight feet over. I murmured a few mild prayers before putting again, and this time I succeeded in sinking the ball, which was a great relief, I can assure you.

In the afternoon I had a much easier time of it, played well, and thought at last I was coming into my game. But Lister Hartley, a fine young English golfer, was too good, and out I went with a bang. Hartley will be a member of this year's British team, and he is a fine golfer, long and straight, and sound in every respect.

I have told you about my matches. There were others that for downright closeness were mighty interesting and in most of these the American players figured prominently. Of course, Bobby Jones was the star attraction and the crowds followed his every move. One of his early matches was with a player named Sid Roper, and he was looked on by the critics as a 'rabbit.' In the eyes of the critics you are either a 'rabbit' or a 'tiger,' the first being a golfer of ordinary ability and the second representing a giant of the game. Well,

Sid Roper, more, I suppose, because he was little known, was a rabbit in the eyes of the spectators.

The match started in a spectacular manner. Two fine tee shots were driven down the fairway and Roper was nearer the hole on the seconds, both well played. Bobby probably was desirous of impressing Roper with his skill at the outset, so he holed a hard twenty-foot putt, downhill, for a three. Roper never batted an eyelash. He barely missed his putt and became one down.

On the fourth hole, Jones hit such a long tee shot that he caught a small trap in the middle of the fairway, and when Roper laid his iron eight feet from the hole, it seemed like a squared match. Bobby went down into the trap with a spade mashie. The hole is over four hundred yards. Jones hit his ball, and it went into the hole for a two. If that bothered Roper, he showed no emotions whatsoever. He kept on plugging away, making hole after hole in fours, and never wavered for a minute. The young man, finally beaten three and two, had made one five and fifteen fours for the sixteen holes played, and he gave a grand exhibition against the deadliest golf he probably had ever seen.

Then there was the match between Tolley and Jones. In a Walker Cup match over the same layout, Jones had annihilated Tolley four years before. Twelve down and eleven to play was the verdict on that occasion. But golfing defeats are quickly forgotten, and what takes place today is no indication of what will happen the next time two golfers meet. Tolley was a worthy opponent. He is like the little girl who, when she is good, she is very, very good, and when she is bad, she is horrid. Tolley was very, very good. So was Bobby, and the eighteen holes found them even. On the nineteenth, Jones stymied Tolley when the latter was three feet from the hole, and that was the finish. With the exception of the close call Bobby had with Tolley and the hard match against Roper, Jones was hitting on high and was the big favorite for the title. Other Americans were mowing partners down with consummate ease, with the United States amateur champion Johnston playing well and George Voigt in magnificent form.

Then came a match between Jones and Johnston. Bobby, playing brilliantly and cashing in on the few Johnston mistakes, soon rolled up a four-hole lead with six to go. Johnston won two of the next three. He also won the seventeenth, and started for the home hole one down. Both hit good tee shots on this simple-looking but troublesome home hole. Both second shots were on the green a long way from the cup. Bobby had to play first, and his approach putt fell nine feet short. Here was Johnston's opportunity. Jones might hole his nine-footer, but the odds were against his doing so. Jimmy made a great approach putt from forty feet and laid his ball stone dead for a sure four. Many of us stood on the balcony of the Grand Hotel, where we could look down on the green and see everything. Bobby seemed worried, as well he should have been, because, after having the match practically won, he had let Johnston get off the hook and now had a curling nine-foot putt to save it.

I was standing near George Von Elm on the balcony. Von Elm remarked as Bobby took his stance, 'Bobby has holed hundreds of putts like that one; he will pop that in.' Jones had putted and out of sight clucked the ball. It was a grand finish to a great match. Voigt continued to win his matches in hollow fashion and he finally arrived at the semi-finals with Bobby. Voigt had been invincible all the week and a classic was expected, and that is exactly what it turned out to be. Voigt is not a long hitter, but St. Andrews was very fast, and whatever advantage Bobby might have had under normal conditions was offset by the fact that Voigt could get sufficient length on the hard ground. Furthermore, Voigt was and is a master with iron clubs, and if there is a better man on the greens, I do not care to see him.

The match started with both men playing splendidly. The first five holes were halved. The fifth, well over five hundred yards, was made in fours by the two golfers, Voigt using an iron for a second, easily reaching the green. Finally Voigt won a hole and became one up. At the thirteenth he came through with another win, thus putting him two holes to the good. The play was brilliant, Voigt slightly outplaying the great Bobby on the second shots to the greens. There is a fable around St. Andrews that says the golfer who is two up and five to play never wins his match. As Jones and Voigt moved toward the fourteenth tee, I heard at least a dozen spectators say Voigt would lose because he was two up and five to play.

The day was unusually calm for St. Andrews, but a fresh wind suddenly blew up which changed the playing conditions tremendously on that long fourteenth. The wind was across, blowing from the water, and neither player could reach the green with two shots. As the gallery hemmed in around the tee, Voigt took his stance. He could not feel the force of the wind. It was strong. He knew he could not get home in two, so he chose the direction down the right side of the fairway. He hit his ball well, but the moment it got into the air it was wafted to the right, over the wall, and out of bounds. Jones saw all this, so he proceeded to hit his drive well to the left and onto the adjoining fifth fairway. Penalty for out of bounds at St. Andrews is stroke and distance; therefore, Voigt had to tee up and play three and never had a look-in for the hole. The fifteenth was halved.

The sixteenth measures about three hundred and fifty or sixty yards with the railroad track on the right-hand side of the fairway. Jones had the honor. He drove a long ball, not down his fairway, but over onto the third, many yards to the left of the line of play. Down the middle around the two-hundred-yard mark are two little pot bunkers, one of which lies in the face of a mound, and can be seen from the tee, and the other just beyond. The mound itself is called the 'Principal's Nose.' Voigt tried to poke his ball to the left of the Principal's Nose, but it had a wee fade, and the next thing we knew the ball was tossed into the trap. Jones's tee shot, which appeared to be very wild, was now seen to be in the safest spot imaginable, proving that he knew the old course at St. Andrews from A to Izzard. He had a difficult pitch to make between a pair of traps near the green, but he succeeded in splitting the distance, landed his ball on the fairway, and it rolled within eight feet of the flag. Voigt had no chance whatsoever, and the match was square at last.

Now they came to the treacherous seventeenth. The wind was still across, and Jones did not dare risk a drive over the barn and the corner of the station-master's garden. He drove out to the left. So did Voigt. Two difficult shots to a difficult green had to be played. George played a risky long iron and his ball barely failed to roll upon the plateau green. Bobby was more conservative, and his second fell twenty yards short. It was obvious he was gambling on his approach.

In front of that seventeenth green is a bank which makes it necessary to play a running approach. It is impossible to pitch to the green, or at least it was the day Jones and Voigt played their match. Bobby's run-up was weak and stopped eighteen feet from the cup. Voigt, on the front edge of the green with the bank to negotiate, used his putter and very nearly holed out for a three. He was stony. Jones was now faced with the dire necessity of having to drop his long putt to keep the match even. He was excited. Ordinarily, he takes a quick squint at the line, steps up and hits his ball. On this occasion he consumed quite a bit of time and looked his line of putt over carefully from every angle. If ever Bobby needed to drop a putt, he needed that one. After unusual care he stepped up and rolled that ball as true as a die into the cup. The crowd went wild as they rushed for the eighteenth.

Again two fine tee shots boomed up or down the fairway. Voigt was away. In front of him was the Valley of Sin. Using a spade mashie, he tried to pitch all the way to the green. His ball started well, but lost speed in flight and failed by six inches to hit the flat part of the green. It caught the undulation and trickled back into the Valley of Sin. Bobby played boldly and got nicely on. I have already told you something about the Valley of Sin in another chapter. Voigt failed to get dead and lost the hole and the match.

It was a tough game to lose. He was not outplayed at any stage, and the only difference in the play of the two was the better judgment exercised by Bobby, whose knowledge of St. Andrews was almost perfect. I was very much impressed with Voigt's remark as he walked off the green. A close friend walked up and said, 'George, that is too bad; I believe you should have won.' Voigt looked at the friend and said, 'Just remember, Al, it's only a golf game, after all.' Certainly a sportsmanlike remark for a loser to make. Little things such as these make the game so wonderful.

CHAPTER XV

A ST. ANDREWS CARD

BOBBY was now in the finals of a championship he wanted to win more than any other. His opponent was Roger Wethered. Saturday was a holiday, and people came from all parts of Scotland to see the two great golfers play the final. It was estimated the gallery was somewhere between fifteen and twenty thousand. An interesting thing happened on the first tee. As the two golfers waited for the gallery to settle, an official of the Royal and Ancient Club, standing near Jones and Wethered, opened with the following: 'Golf has been played at St. Andrews for over a hundred years. During that time every one of the greatest golfers in the world has at some time or other played the Old Course. Wonderful scores have been made, but no one has ever been able to play a round without having at least one five on his card.' I was standing very close to Bobby, and I saw his mouth tighten a bit, but he never said a word. The pair were called to the tee and they drove off.

Wethered and Jones were in great fettle as the fours were rattled off without a hitch. Bobby picked up a three on one of the early holes, which was offset by a four on the par three eighth, and at the end of nine holes the match, the final of the British amateur championship, was square, with each out in 35. Then Jones put on the pressure. With a string of fours, broken by a couple of threes, Bobby stood on the seventeenth tee five up, with two holes left of the morning round. The drives to the seventeenth were letter-perfect. Wethered had to take a chance and, playing a spoon, he hit a grand shot that landed and stayed on the narrow putting surface. Bobby also used a spoon, but he had a little too much draw on his shot, and it curled off toward the end of its flight and caught the tricky little trap on the edge of the green. There was nothing much the matter with the manner in which he played the stroke because, while trapped, the ball was not more than fifteen or twenty feet from the hole. From his position in the trap, Jones had the meanest sort of a shot to play. Just over the edge of the trap, the green sloped away sharply, and it was fast. He was approaching the hole at the narrowest point of the green and there was grave danger of overrunning it and going into the road. There was little sand, which made an explosion shot almost out of the question. I watched him take his swing, noticed he cut the legs from under the ball, saw it come up and barely clear the top of the bank. Then it hit on the down slope and suddenly began to twist and squirm. There was so much backspin on the ball that hit the down slope that it stopped almost instantly, and then trickled past the cup a scant two feet. What a shot! I was standing near an old St. Andrews player, and he said it was the finest shot he had ever seen. Wethered made a fine putt of eighteen feet that stopped on the edge. Bobby hurriedly took his stance and just as hurriedly hit his ball and — horrors! He missed. Missed the two-foot putt. He whaled his drive a mile up the eighteenth fairway. He was mad! The four he got won the hole, and he was five up again with eighteen holes remaining, the championship as good as won.

I crossed the street to the Grand Hotel and went to his room with him. He was wild. He looked at me with disgust, and I could not understand his attitude. 'What in the world has got into you, Bobby? You are five up,' I said. He answered, 'Did you hear what that official said on the first tee?' I thought a moment. 'And I had to miss a two-foot putt to be the first man to play St. Andrews without taking a five.' I believe that incident on the first tee had whipped Bobby into an unbeatable frame of mind, and he was concentrating so intently on the fours he was making that it was responsible for the magnificent caliber of his golf.

After luncheon he went to work again. The crowd lined both sides of the fairway, and a tremendous crowd gathered in back of the green. I have never seen anything to equal the size of that gallery, and it was possible only to see a shot now and then. I happened to be one of Bobby's marshals, along with George Von Elm, Tom Paine, and Sherwood Hirt from Atlanta, and it was all we could do to keep Jones from being stampeded to death. Bobby kept adding a hole here and there, until the twelfth green was reached, and that is where the match ended. And such a demonstration! The gallery rushed madly onto the green and Bobby turned white as they surged forward. He is a great favorite, and in 1927, when he won the British open, also at St. Andrews, his victory met with such popular favor, that he was raised to the shoulders of a group and carried all over the place. He was fearful of a repetition, and he knew his limbs were in danger of being torn from his body.

As a further example of the crowd, let me say that Henry Lapham was standing on the edge of a trap not far from the green, and when the winning putt was made, Henry was rushed off his feet, and the next thing he knew he was in the bottom of the trap with many feet trampling over him. Please do not misunderstand me when I relate these incidents, as meaning the crowd was hostile. They were desirous only of paying tribute to Jones whom they admired so much. Bobby never forgot him-

self. He turned to me as the crowd rushed toward
him, and said, 'Francis, please look after Roger.'
I did the best I could under the conditions, and
four mounted policemen — or maybe they were
not mounted — escorted the winner back to the
clubhouse.

That was the start of a record which I doubt
will ever be equaled, that of winning all four major
championships in a single year, the British amateur
and open and the United States open and amateur.
I did not see Bobby play at Hoylake, so I know
nothing of what took place there. Likewise, I did
not see him win our open at Interlaken. However,
when we started into play at Merion for the
amateur championship, every golfer and spectator
hoped nothing would happen to spoil his record.
Bobby took care of that incidental himself. The
rest of us reminded me of a one-act show. We
represented the chorus, or the scenery, or something, and the act was started.

Crowds followed Bobby before the championship
and all through it. In one of the qualifying rounds,
Wood Platt, the witty Philadelphian, was harassed
time and again by the spectators. On one hole,
quite out of patience, Wood requested some spectators to move out of the way. He was informed
that they were waiting for Bobby Jones to come
along. 'I know all about it,' said Platt, 'but would
you mind stepping aside until I play this shot?

You know you will have all the week to watch Bobby.'

In the championship at Merion, apart even from Bobby's success, which I believe was the hardest of the four because of its importance, there were many interesting games. The qualifying round is always a nerve-racking thing. 'Jimmy' Johnston was the defending champion and his first medal round was 83. That was a heart-breaker. He came back strong the second day with a 73, but the fine come-back was not good enough, because he missed the play-off by one stroke. I think eleven players participated in the play-off for seven or eight places, and among others were Chick Evans, Jesse Sweetser, and Phillip Finlay. The eleven were sent away in one group of six and another of five, to play what amounts to a sudden-death affair.

In the first group Finlay dropped a great putt for a three, and so got in. Sweetser was in a group that had to rise early in the morning and play the long second hole. So, too, was Maurice McCarthy, I believe, although my memory is a bit hazy about him. Evans was the unlucky one in his group, or rather he was one of the unlucky ones. He had a fine drive and a gorgeous iron fifteen feet from the hole. It was getting dark, and there is always a certain amount of confusion attending a play-off. The referee has to be careful to follow the play of each man and order them to play in turn in so far as the distance from the hole is concerned. Evans was one of the last to be called upon to play. Two putts from fifteen feet would suffice. He putted his first eighteen inches from the cup, and then rested while the others holed out. When it came time for him to play, it was dark, and he failed to see a slight roll, missed his putt, and was out.

I am almost sure McCarthy was one of those who was in the play-off, and I will tell you why. He got up early with the remaining players in the tie, succeeded in lasting through the play-off of one hole, and then went on to win a nineteen-hole match. That gave him the privilege of meeting George Von Elm in the second round, about which I will write later.

In my first match-play round I was called upon to meet Charles Koscis, an eighteen-year-old boy from Detroit. I took one look at the way he hit his drive on the first hole, and I made up my mind I was in for something. I played a second shot six feet from the cup. He was on the green on his second, and then holed a twenty-five-footer for a three. I wish to say I do not know how I dropped that six-footer for a half. I won the fourth hole after the first three had been halved, and then Charlie went to work. For the next twelve holes he was three better than an average of fours, and I was on my way home so far as the championship was concerned.

A Game of Golf

Bill McPhail, one of my playmates of earlier days, was in a tussle with a young New York school lad, named Sidney Noyes. Bill had evened the match on the eighteenth. After two good tee shots down the first fairway, Noyes overpitched the green and went out of bounds. The penalty was stroke and distance. McPhail played cautiously and won the match. He came over to me, and I have always been interested in chatting to players after they have had a hard battle. 'Well done, Bill,' was my opening remark. 'You know that second shot of Noyes's was the best I have ever seen,' was Bill's reply, and I knew how he felt.

Phil Perkins was beaten in an early round and so, too, was George Voigt, the chap who had played so well abroad. Practically all the Walker Cup players were eliminated in the first or second round, with the exception of Jones and Von Elm, which only goes to prove that anything can happen in golf. Then the word was flashed that Von Elm was having a tough match with McCarthy and was about to be finished off at the eighteenth. McCarthy was leading one up, and after the two had driven well, Mac placed a second three or four feet from the edge of the green, a spot from which he was almost bound to hole out in two more. Von Elm was plumb on and not far from the cup. McCarthy chipped weakly and left himself a seven-footer. Von Elm hit the cup for a three, but the ball refused to drop. Then Maurice missed, and the match was square and away to the extra holes.

I shall live a long time before I see a better exhibition of golf than I saw in the twilight of that beautiful September evening. Sound fours halved the first. On the second, Von Elm hooked his brassie shot to the rough and then overplayed the green into a trap. Maurice played two great shots and put his third on the green. This green is peculiarly constructed. The fairway runs into the green which is level for eight or ten feet. Then there is a dip, and on the other side of the dip, the green runs up again to a plateau. McCarthy's ball on the approach had run down the dip and up again to the plateau, which left him a mighty difficult approach putt, from about thirty feet. Von Elm got out of the trap, but was so far from the hole that the best he could do was a six. Mac putted from the upper part of the green to within three or four feet and then missed the putt which would have given him the match. The hole was halved in six.

The situation was reversed on the short third. This time Von Elm had a putt not longer than two feet to win. He missed. On the long three-shot fourth, both had reasonable putts for better than par fours. The fifth is a stiff two-shotter. McCarthy was on the front edge of the green in two. Von Elm was well on and ten feet from the hole. Mac putted his thirty-footer an inch from the hole and, taking the roll of the green into consideration, that putt surely traveled forty-five feet — a perfect rainbow. George was unequal to the task of dropping the ten-footer and the match continued to the sixth extra. Here once again was a stout two-shot hole. It is a hole where a four is a real accomplishment and a five never to be sneezed at. The two game players cracked drives down the middle and fine shots to the green, this time with Mac nearest the pin. Again the hole was halved. The seventh found Von Elm with the advantage. His second was hole-high eight feet from the cup. Mac pulled his mashie slightly and the ball trickled off the green into short rough, but a delicately played chip shot placed the ball dead. Again Von Elm missed. At this stage it seemed as though some one player, and they were taking turns, *must* drop a holable putt, because they were sticking their balls close on almost every approach.

The eighth brought about another halved hole. To the short ninth Von Elm was eight feet away and Mac about twelve. Mac putted, hit the hole, and as the ball turned off, it stymied Von Elm, and that hole was halved. Bear in mind this was the ninth extra hole and McCarthy had already played one hole in the morning to qualify in the play-off, then nineteen to win his first match, making twenty holes played altogether during the morning; then twenty-seven so far in the Von Elm match.

The tenth hole at Merion is one of those terrible affairs, a great hole, which compels the golfer to place his tee shot with relation to the short approach he must execute to a narrow and tremendously trapped green. The drives could not have been better placed by hand. They were to the right and long and right up the opening. McCarthy was away. He played a pitch-and-run shot that caught the turf perfectly, rolled along to the green, and continued on until it stopped — six inches from the cup. Par was four. Von Elm is a fighter. He knew he had to counter with a brilliant shot, and that is what he played. His ball was eight feet from the hole. He had not holed a single putt, and he was due. It was quite dark, and there was no chance to play another hole that day. He studied his line, putted, but the ball did not have 'legs,' and slipped off as it died just short of the goal. That settled the longest scratch match within knowledge, and the winner, Maurice McCarthy, had played exactly forty-eight holes on that Wednesday. You may imagine he had had enough golf for that day.

The championship sifted down to a final between Gene Homans and Bobby Jones. It is not doing Gene an injustice, I hope, to say Bobby was a ten-to-one favorite, and he came through in a blaze of glory. Gene was good, but Bobby was better, and that about sums up the story. Homans did the best he could against the greatest golfer who ever lived, but catching Bobby in a final is not my idea of a soft assignment. At about that stage of a championship he is positively unbeatable, and he can make you so sick of seeing drives and irons that travel nowhere but on the straightest line between the tee and the green that you are helpless.

Shortly after that championship meeting, two announcements were made that staggered the American golfing public. The first, that was to remove from amateur golf in this country a great golfer, was George Von Elm's decision to become a business man golfer. Von Elm was tired of chasing around, here, there, and everywhere, competing as an amateur. He was always a serious threat, and while he succeeded in winning the championship in 1926, I suppose I am safe in saying he did not always enjoy the success his brilliant play justified. He had been a thorn in the side of the professionals in open competition and could always be counted upon to finish among the first four or five in medal competition, knocking at the door, but not quite getting through. His record was a remarkable one when one considers that he was living in the age of Jones, Hagen, Sarazen, Mac Smith, Farrell, Diegel, and others.

The American public had just assimilated the

news of Von Elm's exit from the amateur ranks when a real bombshell was tossed into their midst. That was the decision of Bobby Jones to retire from competitive golf. Knowing Bobby as I believe I do, I do not think he was actuated by the monetary end which came later. I may be in error in expressing the following opinion, because I have never discussed the matter with Bobby at all. In 1926, I happen to know, a motion-picture executive approached Bobby with a proposal, whereby Bobby was to make a motion picture, and he had his option of accepting a substantial emolument or designating a charity to receive it in case he did not wish to profit personally. Before the proposition even reached the formative state, Bobby turned to the proposer and said, 'I am not interested in any proposition you may offer.' His tone of voice was indicative of his feelings, and the matter was dropped forthwith without the usual persuasive conversations that such affairs generate.

My opinion is this: I think Bobby Jones was so fed up on galleries, excitement, and notoriety which comes under the heading of publicity, that he was sick and tired of it all. There is great satisfaction in playing in and winning golf championships but when the appetite has been whetted and satisfied, then a fellow likes to sneak off by himself in a friendly fourball match and have some fun. He does not want to feel that his very life depends upon the playing of a perfect shot. He wants some kind of relaxation. I have played quite a bit of golf with Bobby Jones, and I have yet to see him start out or finish without a stream of people trailing him. I know of one or two rounds he has played where he was just in the company of his friends, and his golf was about as dufferish as it could be, but he had the thrill of his lifetime because, as he himself said, he did not think golf could be played so badly. That was not the Jones who astounded two continents by the everlasting flow of perfect strokes that left his clubs. I think he wants to golf with friends in a friendly way and without the blare of the trumpets and the excitement of the tournament.

CHAPTER XVI

'THIS LOOKS LIKE A FATHER-AND-SON TOURNAMENT'

Now that Jones and Von Elm were definitely out, the championship took on a different aspect. We had a new ball to contend with, for one thing, and I am not going to say a word for or against the large and light ball, which George Duncan called 'Larger, Lighter, and Lousier,' at a dinner once. Forgive me, please, George, for telling tales out of school. The first thought that came to my mind when the big ball was launched was this: It is here and I shall have to like it. After all, it is not the ball, but the game, that counts, so long as the powers that be give us something to hit. Removing Bobby and George Von Elm filled everyone with the idea that 'he' had a chance to win the championship. When we gathered at the Beverly Country Club in 1931, the locker room was busy with players young and old, all figuring they stood a chance of winning — and surely they did, too.

Why, do you know Watts Gunn came to me and said, 'Francis, I feel like a new person altogether with Bobby and George out of the way.' That was the atmosphere everywhere. From a psychological point of view, if nothing else, I had an advantage, because almost everyone I met at Chicago was

241

fussing about the light ball. Still, they had to play it. I never gave the ball a great deal of thought. I had been playing well and hoped to continue. I wanted to win the championship a second time and devoted my time and effort toward this thought. I had long got over the idea that this was to be the year. I figured I was not too old. I knew I had the stamina although friends doubted this. It was a question of ability, and not stamina. You always look and act tired in a competitive golf match if you are not performing up to normal.

I had never seen the Beverly layout, so as usual I planned to arrive at the scene in time to spend a couple of days on the course. We landed in Chicago on a Friday, and my intention was to play one round Friday and two on Saturday, resting on Sunday. I am one of those chaps who feel you can do more harm by intensive practice than by too little. One has to do some gambling, and why not gamble that you will qualify, and ease by two matches on the shy side of playing form. It is easier to come up to form than to get there quickly and have to stay there. In other words, if you can squeeze by two matches with fair golf, the chances are you will improve from there on. If you are playing at top for the first two rounds, the chances are you will slip a bit later, and that is just when you cannot afford to slip.

A FATHER-AND-SON TOURNAMENT

I had been playing well around Boston, and prior to leaving for Chicago I played a match against George Von Elm and Billy Burke, with Guilford as a partner. Aside from a few friendly matches, it was the only serious competition I indulged in. Guilford and I won that match by three up and two to play, and it was just the necessary preparation for it furnished me with the confidence that I was hitting the ball well, a mighty helpful asset. And the day before leaving for the amateur championship, I played a game late in the afternoon at the Brae-Burn Country Club with my good friend Melvin Heath and his two boys. We did not begin our play until nearly five o'clock, and it was just the sort of game that I like to play — one where there is plenty of conversation and nothing serious at stake. Thoroughly relaxed, I hit my drive straight down the middle of the fairway and pitched a second a foot from the hole, which gave me a three. I did the same on the next. After two good fours, I made another on the long fifth, by pitching my third stone dead. The sixth hole is short, and in front of the green is a brook. My mashie shot hit the bank and rolled back to the water's edge. From here I chipped with a niblick near enough to get my three, and was away to a flying start.

The seventh is a testing two-shotter, and my long iron rolled overboard to the bank. I did not take any particular pains with the shot, but when the chip stopped, it was in the bottom of the cup for another three. On the eighth, which was a one-shotter, I reached the green, but took three putts. A long putt went in on the ninth for a three, and I was out in 31. It was one of those amusing stretches where everything went right and without strain. The card read as follows: 3–3–4–4–4–3–3–4–3. Coming home, I finished with a 36 and an eighteen hole total of 67.

To get back to Beverly. The course was very long and well trapped, and after an eighteen-hole trip I decided it was one of those tests where putting was to be a great factor, along with accurate tee-shot hitting. During the practice rounds the holes had been placed near the front edges of the greens for the purpose of saving the choice spots for the championship. After playing two holes, I made up my mind that there was nothing to be gained by playing for the pins, so I planned my practice round as follows: After each tee shot I chose the club that would fetch me to the middle of the green, regardless of where the pin was placed, and I paid no attention whatever to a score. Hole after hole I played for the centers of the greens, and then putted casually at the hole, caring little whether or not I got the par on the hole.

The ninth green in particular was devoid of

grass, and the hole was cut six feet from the near edge of the green. My second shot landed me in the middle of the green, and my first putt, downhill, rolled ten feet off the putting surface. That same condition existed throughout the round, but I had learned what the range was to the center of the greens, and, after all, that is what I wanted to learn. Saturday we practiced under the same conditions, and the wind blew a gale. I was seeing Beverly, you might say, at its worst. I had originally planned to finish my practice session on Sunday, but it blew so hard I decided there was nothing to be gained, and that I must take the chance of learning some more about the course in the medal rounds. Therefore, I took in a baseball game.

I felt the scoring would be moderately high because the course was playing long and the greens at the time were not in their best shape. For five holes I played well, and then on the par three sixth I ran into a five, which was costly, since the seventh and ninth holes were long and a five was the best to expect on each of these. The first nine was made in forty strokes, which was only fair golf, and left me little leeway to qualify unless I perked up noticeably in my play. A par three followed by a par five on the long eleventh was satisfactory, and then we reached the little twelfth.

In front of the tee was a pond. Just beyond the pond were several traps. Then the green, set up nicely, and beyond the green, long grass. I pitched with a mashie niblick eighteen inches from the cup and got my two, which started me on the way. I can remember, after making that two, of thinking that if I stuck to par on the last six holes I should be back in 34, for a round of 74. Therefore, I concentrated severely on each hole, made them all in par, and had my 74. The second day, I scored 78, which was one of those rounds where I was never in trouble, and could have saved several strokes with a bit of care. In other words, my play justified a lower score, but it was good enough to qualify me without trouble, and that is what I wanted.

Some of the other boys had plenty of bother. Chick Evans, for instance, was playing splendidly, and with four holes left on his second round was almost a sure qualifier. He took three putts on the fifteenth, three on the sixteenth, missed the green to the seventeenth, and then took three more putts, and was finally left with a five to tie for last place with many others. Never shall I forget that great golfer on the last putting green. Three splendid shots, a drive, brassie, and mashie put him exactly twelve feet from the hole. A host of players had tied for the last place, with totals of 156. There were something like seven positions open, so Evans's situation was not altogether a hopeless one. If he could hole that putt, he was in without the play-off. Two putts meant a play-off. There was never a greater golfer than Evans when it came to driving and iron-club play, but all that good work was frequently wasted because of wretched putting. This time he fell three feet short of the cup on his first putt, and then missed again. He had taken three putts on the last four greens and had failed by one stroke. But that is golf. In the locker room, Chick was the most disappointed man I have ever seen. He had pointed to this championship and then, as often before, his putter turned on him.

There were others, too. 'Jimmy' Johnston, far from his best health, failed to qualify. So, too, did Max Marston, Cyril Tolley, and Phil Perkins, and any one of these chaps was quite capable of playing well enough to win the title. Another lad who fell by the wayside was Charley Kocsis, the schoolboy from Detroit who had put me out at Merion the year before and had rolled up an impressive record in Michigan, where in a play-off for the State open title he had beaten Tommy Armour, British open champion, by one stroke. One can never tell about this game of golf. Kocsis has a beautiful swing and is a sound golfer all the way through. It does not seem possible, but it is a fact, that he played fourteen holes without making a hole in par, and his first round of 87 put him definitely out. It is to his credit that he had the courage to go out the second day and score a 74 when he had no chance of qualifying.

At least seventeen of the thirty-two qualifiers reached the match-play rounds for the first time in their golfing careers, and it was certainly a wide-open proposition, with the youngsters dominating the play. In a tie for first place were Yates, the gigantic Rochester star, Charley Seaver, and John Lehman, the latter earning his honors by tripping around the course in a downpour in 70 strokes, a brilliant score over a tough course.

The very first round saw the elimination of two warm favorites. Billy Howell, a light-haired nineteen-year-old lad from Richmond, Virginia, disposed of Goodman. Goodman is a great golfer and was the boy who stopped Jones at Pebble Beach in 1929. Then Richard Martin from· Chicago knocked out George Voigt, another favorite, by two up and one to play. My opponent in the first round was John Shields from Seattle, and thanks to steadiness through the fairways and a few good putts at critical spots, I succeeded in winning my first match by four and three.

In the lower half a great match was staged between the co-medalists, Seaver and Yates, featured by much erratic golf and many brilliant recoveries. Both Yates and Seaver are notoriously long from the tees, and they set out to smash the ball as far as possible. Seaver was extremely wild, and in the end it was this factor that cost him the match. The other medalist, John Lehman, after reaching the turn three holes to the good on Paul Jackson, suddenly lost his effectiveness and was beaten by a hole. So you can see the championship was beginning as one of upsets and surprises.

It was my lot to take on Frank Connolly in round number two, and I was prepared for a battle. Often a fine young player will shoot his head off for one round and then, owing to inexperience or the lack of competitive testing, run into a streak of erratic play which brings about his downfall. I could afford to take no chances and settled down to a program of hitting the ball as well as I could and let this stand up against whatever my opponent might produce. Therefore, I simply tried to keep my ball out of trouble, and contented myself with the thought that at some stages of our match he would offer opportunities for me to win holes and when they appeared I was to take full advantage of them. I could see by Connolly's swing that he could play well. However, his morning round was at such a furious pace — he had beaten Moreland with a round of 71 — it was natural to expect him to let down a bit, and that is just what happened. On the first four holes he erred somewhere along the line, slipped a stroke to par on each, and I became four up. After halving the fifth, I won the sixth. A lead of five holes in an eighteen-hole round is an almost impossible barrier to hurdle, and this is how we stood at the end of nine holes.

He holed a two on the tenth, but wins on the next two put me in a safe position, and I coasted home a winner by five and four.

I reached the clubhouse just in time to avoid a drenching rain that came down on a sudden, and after changing my clothes I walked out to the eighteenth green to see the finish of the match between Paul Jackson and Fred Wright, the winner of which was to be my opponent in the third round. It was raining as hard as I had ever seen it. Jackson and Wright were all even playing the home hole, and the green resembled a miniature of Niagara Falls, as the water rushed from the topmost part of the green in a sheet down the incline. Jackson was short in three, Wright in a trap. Then in that deluge the two tried to get their balls into the cup. There was not a dry spot on that green, and therefore there was little sense in taking advantage of the casual water ruling which permitted the player to place his ball so as not to putt through water. If the situation had not been so serious, it would have been funny, because Jackson, after six shots had been played, finally placed his ball near enough to the hole to sink his next shot. In the meantime Wright had maneuvered his ball to within two feet of the cup and had the putt for a half. The water gushed over the hole in such a manner that Wright had to use his hand to scoop the water out of the hole so that he might see it.

After perhaps a delay of five minutes, he hit his putt, missed, and Jackson won the hole and the match with a seven.

Now I had another youngster to play against, and it was at thirty-six holes.

When Paul Jackson and I met for the first time on the tee at Beverly, there was a good-sized gallery waiting to see our match. I remember well my impressions. Jackson is twenty years of age, pink-cheeked and fine-looking. As we drove off the tee straight down the middle of the fairway, we walked together and breaking through the crowd, I heard a spectator say, 'This looks like a father-and-son tournament.' I suppose the gray hairs around my temples gave me a paternal aspect alongside of the much younger-looking boy I was playing. However, a golf match is no time or place to think of such things, and I decided to play the same sort of game against Jackson that was successful in my match with Connolly. You can afford to lie in wait for opportunities in contests of thirty-six holes, where it is dangerous over the shorter route.

The first five holes were halved, four of which were played in par figures and the other in one over. Then four more holes played in par gave me a lead at the turn of four up. This lead was increased to six at the end of the eighteen, and, unless I blew wide open or Jackson hit a patch of unbeatable golf, I had the match in hand. My score for the round of 74 was made up of steady play, the brand of golf that usually wins matches because of the fact that few openings are left to an opponent. As a matter of interest, I lost but one hole in the morning. At the twenty-seventh I had run the margin to eight, and it was simply a question of hanging on. Jackson is a stout little fighter, and he never gave up, winning the tenth and eleventh in par. However, a pitch one foot from the cup on the short twelfth ended my activities for that day at least.

For the eighth time in my golfing career I had reached the semi-final round of the amateur championship. Again I was drawn against a youngster, Billy Howell. I had played well and won my first three matches with consistent golf from the tee to the green, and my confidence was increasing with each round. But you can never tell a thing about these young lads. One minute they give you a chance to cash in on a mistake, and when you are all set, they will knock you galley west with a long putt or a deadly pitch. In the morning I played erratically, by far the worst round I had, and Howell was one up.

If you can get off with a poor round and find yourself but one down, there is much to be thankful for, because you have the feeling that your game will return on the next start. I gave the match much thought during the lunch hour, picked out the shots that had given me the most trouble, and made up my mind to correct the faults that afternoon. I was swinging my iron clubs too quickly, mistiming many of them, and that was the thing that had got me into my difficulties.

Playing the first hole in the afternoon, after a fine drive, I hit what appeared to be a decent approach, but the ball struck a hard spot and rolled over the green and well down the embankment. That cost me the hole. This put me two down. Then Billy softened up a bit, and I won four of the next five and became two up. We were now playing the long seventh. My drive was long and straight. Howell sliced his ball far to the right, but since the green was well beyond reach in two shots there was no point in striving for distance. Billy played back to the fairway, and directly after, I banged a brassie shot straight down the fairway. Howell was short of the green with his third and my ball in three rested twelve feet past the hole. Howell played an exquisite chip shot a foot from the hole and had recovered a stroke that seemed gone. As I sighted my putt, I noticed a ridge a yard in front of my ball. Beyond the ridge the green sloped sharply down to the hole. I could ill-afford to go for my putt because the green was fast and to do so would be flirting with danger. Therefore, I decided to tap my ball as easily as possible and be satisfied with a half in five. Then I gave thought

253

to the ridge. I must hit my ball hard enough to negotiate this, and then depend upon the weight of the ball to carry it along. In my anxiety to putt over the ridge, I stroked the ball too firmly and to my chagrin I watched it slide by the hole and stop six feet below the cup and directly in back of Howell's ball — a dead stymie. Of course, I failed to negotiate the stymie and lost the hole.

Frequently in close matches an experience of this kind is calamitous. As I teed up my ball, I said to myself that Howell will probably do something that will make me never forget that seventh green. He did. He rolled a long putt into the cup on the eighth green for a win, and we were all square. I got a hole back on the ninth and started away on the last nine with the slim lead of one up against a fighting golfer. The match was squared again on the tenth and the eleventh was halved. On the short twelfth, Billy rocked me off my feet by sinking a long putt for a two. This match was getting hot, and I knew I had the fight of my life on my hands. In the first place, I had always felt my friends back home thought I could not get through a semi-final match because of my lack of stamina. To me this was like waving a red flag at a bull. My defeats in the semi-final matches have been the result of better play on the part of my opponents and not through any lack of stamina. And yet I have returned to Boston from champion-

ships and my close friends have said, good-
naturedly, 'Just a semi-finalist.' All these things
were running through my head.

There have been moments in my golfing life
when I could count on a shot to pull me through,
maybe a putt, and I was determined to pull myself
up to this frame of mind. A friend came to me, but
I pushed him aside. I was aroused. Billy Howell
was a grand little fellow, but I wanted to win that
match and had to if for no other reason than to
satisfy those who thought I was worn out that I
could come back. We both reached the thirteenth
green with drives and pitches. Howell was away
and putted stone dead. I was twenty feet from
the cup with a curling putt. I examined every inch
of that roll. I might not have a better chance to
square the match than right here. I took my stance
and the moment I felt the ball on the face of the
putter, I was satisfied. That ball took the various
rolls and turns necessary and ended up in the bottom of the tin.

That was a good start. If Billy Howell was going
to win the match he must earn it. I was not going
to give it to him. We halved the fourteenth.

The fifteenth hole measures four hundred and
forty-eight yards, and it was played into a stiff
wind with no roll to be got on the heavy fairway.
We both hit good drives. Howell shoved his brassie
second far to the right in the rough. I smacked a

brassie on a line for the flag, and because of the low flight of the ball I fully expected a roll which would carry it to the green. It so happened that the ground was soft and my ball stopped ten yards short of the green. Billy had to play over some trees from the rough, and I was confident I could chip close enough to get a four, which might win the hole. Howell, still game, played a gorgeous pitch safely over the trees and his ball stopped fifteen feet from the hole. I wanted to chip with a number three iron, but owing to the fact that the front edge of the fairway near the green was soggy from the rains, I had to give up the idea. I chose a mashie, did not hit my ball firmly, and fell ten feet shy. That was a golden opportunity wasted, but I still had confidence in my putter. Howell just did miss his four, and then it was squarely up to me. Again that good old putter stroked the ball into the cup. I was one up now and full of fight.

Our drives sped down the fairway. Howell hit a long iron to the green. On the right edge was a bank, and any ball that hit the bank must be thrown into the green. A shot directed at the pin might curl to the left and finish in a trap. I was going to give that trap as wide a berth as possible, so I deliberately smashed a number three iron for the bank. Some spectators thought I was lucky to see my ball hit high on the banking and then kick onto the green, but that is just what I expected, and it came off. Howell putted dead and placed his ball between mine and the hole. There was plenty of room, however, to putt around the ball and the roll of the green lessened the danger of duplicating my performance of the seventh, where I stymied myself. In my eagerness to putt around his ball, I neglected to hit the ball firmly, and to my horror I nearly blocked myself off once more. I wasted no time in looking the four-foot putt over. I am in the habit of putting quickly, but I never putted a ball more quickly than that one. It ran into the hole like a scared rabbit, and that hole was halved.

Came the one-shot seventeenth of exactly two hundred yards. Up to now I had been unable to reach that green, which was small and well-trapped, and it was with many misgivings I picked out a number two iron, a club I had played badly, but nevertheless the club for that shot. I never lifted my head after hitting the ball until I knew it was well on its way. When I did look up, it was to see that ball traveling for the middle of the green. It hit the soft turf and died almost instantly. Howell was not so fortunate. He failed to connect with his ball solidly and it drifted to the right and caught a trap. Experience had taught me to expect a brilliant recovery and I was well prepared for what occurred. Billy waded into the sand and blasted his ball out of the trap and almost into

257

the hole. As I looked the line of my putt over, my thoughts wandered to the last hole. I had another rolling putt of twenty feet. I was sure I could put it dead and just as sure the hole would be halved. I putted as gently as I dared to over the skiddy surface, and you can imagine my pleasure at seeing my ball scamper into the cup. It happened so quickly I was stunned, but the match was mine and that is all there was to it. I can recall thinking to myself as Howell entered the trap, just before his grand recovery, how I should play the eighteenth hole, so you see the putt I dropped for the two came most unexpectedly. But then that is one of the fascinating things about golf.

CHAPTER XVII

SEVENTEEN YEARS AFTER

Now I was in the final round, and the main thought was to win. Experience has taught me also that one of the prime requisites of championship play is a well-rested body and mind. All through the week I had retired early, and to this alone I attribute most of my success. There was another factor. Mrs. Lee Mida, a very fine golfer, lives in the Chicago district, and through friends I had the pleasure of meeting her. Her home was rather close to my hotel, and Mrs. Mida placed at my disposal her automobile, radio-equipped, and in this I rode to and from Beverly each day. She was a woman with considerable tournament experience and understood the idiosyncrasies of a person who was trying to win the national amateur golf title. I can never thank Mrs. Mida enough for her kindness and consideration. She drove our party to and from the club each day. If I felt like talking, she was willing to talk with me. Many times, after a hard day, I preferred quiet, in which event the radio was turned on, and we enjoyed the news flashes or a musical program, all of which took much of the strain from the day's play.

When the morning of the final arrived, Mrs.

Mida was at the hotel door early and there was no last-minute rush for Beverly. Arriving well ahead of schedule, I was able to hit a few balls as a warming-up process, and therefore my nerves were quiet and I did not feel in the least excited. It was very windy, at which I was pleased because I felt confident I could navigate the big light ball with some degree of skill over the Beverly course. I had all the respect in the world for the game of my opponent Jack Westland, for, although I had never played with or against him, his scoring was of such a high caliber I should have been foolish to underestimate his ability. By all odds the hardest stretch of the course was the first nine, and Jack played it in 33 his first qualifying round, and no one touched that score. Further, any player who could do this was good enough to do almost anything, so I respected his game thoroughly.

The wind blew across the first fairway from left to right. Having the honor, I drove straight and well down the fairway. Jack sliced his ball, and the wind did the rest, for it was blown yards off the line of play into the rough. His second landed in a trap to the right of the green, and here was an opportunity at the outset that must be taken advantage of. Therefore, with great care I hit a mashie shot that landed and stopped six feet from the hole. That put me one up.

The second hole measures five hundred and

forty yards, played into the same cross-wind, and the only problem offered was that of keeping my ball in fair territory. We both reached this long hole in three, with Westland away. He putted from forty feet stone dead. I was thirty-five feet from the cup. I hit my ball firmly and had the satisfaction of seeing it drop for a better than par four, and I was two up. As I teed my ball on the third tee, I was bound and determined to hold a lead over my opponent, but determination does not always guide the ball accurately and I missed the green to lose that hole. I won the fourth and fifth, and thereafter held the whip hand for the remainder of the first nine, which ended in my favor by four up. This placed me in a fairly secure position, one that permitted me to lie in wait for opportunities. Perhaps owing to a temporary letdown in concentration, I held myself open to errors here and there, and the four-hole lead was reduced to two at the conclusion of thirteen holes.

It was getting serious. After we both had driven and pitched well to the fourteenth green, I ran down a thirty-foot putt for a three, which won a most important hole, in my opinion the vital hole of the match. When an opponent has succeeded in coming from four down to two down, he begins to think that the match is not beyond him and he becomes a harder man to beat than ever. Westland had come from behind and was beginning to find his confidence until that putt of mine dropped in. It was a life-saver. It furnished me, too, with the desire to buckle down to business again, with the result that an iron shot six or seven feet from the four hundred and forty-eight yard fifteenth put me back to four up. On the sixteenth, my friend the putter came to my rescue once more, for, after being outplayed all the way, a putt of thirty-five feet was held for a half.

I won the seventeenth to gain another hole and increase the lead to five holes, at which we retired for luncheon. It was then a case of hanging on, and my mind drifted back home to my children, Barbara and Janice. I reminisced a bit about other championships, thought of matches that I had tossed away, the years of disappointments, and mostly the fact that I dearly wanted to prove to my friends that I did have the necessary stamina to go through. Then, as the years had slipped by, there was that dreadful feeling that we all hate to get, that of thinking we have lost our skill, in short, have outlived our usefulness — in my case, perhaps the idea that I had seen my best days. Indeed, I could think of dozens of things that fired in me the ambition once again to scale the heights. There was no Bobby Jones to hurdle, which, with due deference to the other fine lads in the championship, was a distinct factor in my favor.

The wind was still whipping away in lively fashion as we started our last eighteen holes. My drive was hooked off the first tee to the rough. Westland sliced his ball badly, but it landed amongst a group of spectators and rebounded back to the fairway, and he won the hole. I came back to win the second, third, and fifth, the fourth being halved, and I was now leading by seven holes with thirteen to play.

A position such as this frequently produces over-confidence, and I fought against this as well as the natural tendency to let down — one of the most fatal of all golfing sins. All week long I had had trouble with the short sixth hole and with few exceptions I had missed the green. It was no different on my last shot at the green, for I missed it by a wide margin, and Westland won the hole. The long seventh was halved and Westland took the eighth by better play. This brought my lead back to five again, and Westland was, so to speak, getting his second wind and becoming dangerous, although I was confident of my game and playing within myself.

The twenty-seventh was the clinching hole so far as I was concerned. The hole measures four hundred and twenty-nine yards in length and is a slight dog-leg, playing from right to left. It was a tough par four, not because of severe trappings, but rather because of the condition of the fairway at the place a well-hit drive ordinarily landed.

A Game of Golf

The turf was heavy and a generous growth of plantain leaves made second shots difficult to play. Westland hit a fine drive down the middle. In striving to get my ball just by the bend in the fairway on the left, I got too much right hand into the shot and the ball drifted high and wide over the row of poplars and left me in a miserable spot. Fortunately, I had room to play over the trees, but the green was beyond the power of a pitching club. I could ill-afford to drop that hole, because of the beneficial effect it would have on Westland, who, having won two straight holes, was in a fair way to notch another. From the rough my number four iron sent the ball over the trees to the fairway fifty yards short of the green. Westland smacked his second to the putting surface, and my test came. The green was thoroughly dried out and hard, and I could not hope to pitch on and hold the ball close to the pin. Therefore, I decided to play a pitch-and-run. I kept my eye on the ball, picked the ball clean, and then watched it strike a yard or two off the edge of the green and then roll fully thirty yards more to within two feet of the cup. Whichever hole previously played may have been the turning-point, this was positively the one that clinched the championship. Westland putted stone dead, the hole was halved, and we entered the final dash of nine holes, I with a lead of five.

264

The end was near at hand. On the short tenth I won with a par three. At last I had the match where I wanted it. The holes would soon run out and my job was to sit tight and just keep going. Par fives on the long eleventh and threes on the twelfth placed me dormie six. There was nothing sensational about our play to the thirteenth, the final hole of the day. Just as I was left with two putts to win the championship at Ekwanok against Jerome Travers, seventeen years before, I had the same thing to do against Westland, and you may believe me when I say I took my two putts as carefully as possible. Almost to the minute, seventeen years to a day, I had won by the same margin.

It is impossible for me to express my real feeling of satisfaction in words. When one has made up his mind to accomplish something and it takes seventeen years to do that something, the satisfaction is tremendous. I had persevered, and in my own mind I had honestly believed I could win that championship.

Winning was gratifying, too, because I felt always that if one took care of his health he could go on playing golf indefinitely, or at least until some physical disability set in. I was also convinced that golf is more of a mental strain than a physical one, and that a clear head untroubled with worries will be of more help in a week of championship play than the strongest physique. Another satis-

265

faction: my two little girls may benefit by my experience. If things go wrong for a certain length of time, I hope they will gain the lesson of the value of not giving up. Golf with me has always been just a game, but a game that can teach splendid lessons. First of all, it teaches self-control — patience — the virtue of accepting unfortunate breaks with the same attitude that one absorbs the more pleasant ones — and many more.

The game has been good to me. It has given me the utmost pleasure, and that whether the score has been in the low seventies or the high nineties. It has taught me to be tolerant of others. It has enabled me to weigh my golfing companions, not in terms of scores but as men. Some of the most enjoyable games I have had have been in the company of friends who have vainly tried to break a hundred. The fact that they failed did not interfere with my own game, and time and again I have established record rounds in the company of high handicap players.

I think it was George Low, an old professional who said, 'Golf is an 'umblin' game.' I learned the truth of those words quite early in my career. It was at Manchester, Vermont, the same course over which I won my first amateur championship. Back in 1912, I had played in a medal competition at Ekwanok, and in a fine field, that included many of the best amateurs in the East, I broke the course record with a 70. It was considered to be quite a performance, and that evening, as we sat around the hotel, a fourball match was promoted in which B. Warren Corkran of Baltimore and Walter J. Travis were to play against Fred Herreshoff and myself. I did my best to keep out of the match, because I felt I should be outclassed, and I did not care to make a fool of myself before a thousand people.

The more stubborn I got, the more persuasive became my friends, their chief argument being that, since I was the holder of the record, I should play. So I did. And I contributed much to that match, as far as amusing the gallery was concerned, but nothing as the partner of Fred Herreshoff. Single-handed and with no assistance from me, he held them even for sixteen holes, with some of the greatest playing I have ever seen and miraculous putting. On the seventeenth, I placed my second eight feet from the hole. Herreshoff in three was just on the green at least thirty feet from the cup. Travis had got a four and Herreshoff, no doubt thinking that if I putted I might perhaps hole the eight-footer, asked me to play. I missed the putt and slipped ten inches beyond, and then missed that. Poor Fred! He allowed his ball to remain on the green while I was putting. After my wretched exhibition, he stepped up and sank his putt for the half.

Then, on the final hole I was the only one on the green in two. Walter J. chipped close enough for his four, and again I took three putts, and we were beaten. I hoped the ground would open and swallow me — but no such luck. Yes, 'Golf is an 'umblin' game.'

THE END

APPENDIX

THEORIES OF THE GAME

THERE is no game that has so many theories or ideas as to the proper methods to be used as the game of golf. Great golfers frequently disagree on certain principles and that is perhaps one of the main reasons why we keep everlastingly at it, grasping each new thought with the hope that perhaps we can solve the mystery. As an example of how confusing theories can be, let us go back to 1913, when Harry Vardon was king. Vardon claimed the club was started back by a roll of the left wrist. This idea was readily accepted, and every last one of us tried to put into practice this theory. It was never disputed, for who would dare criticize the invincible Vardon.

Then, exactly ten years later, George Duncan, another great player, openly disagreed with Vardon's theory. And he had as a helpmate, the motion pictures. Films had been taken to substantiate Duncan's argument, and the pictures clearly bore out or favored Duncan's views. He claimed the club was started backward, not by a roll of the left wrist, as Vardon said, but rather a press of the left wrist against the wrist of the right

269

hand. There was no disputing this new thought, because there it was on the silver screen. When Bobby Jones came along to start his marvelous reign of supremacy, it was noticed that Bobby had developed to a perfect degree that preliminary press of the left wrist. It is now generally accepted as the correct manner of starting the clubhead backward.

Once the back swing has been started, the next thought of importance is that of the stiff left arm. My observations have convinced me that every first-class golfer does keep his left arm straight until such time as the left elbow must bend to permit the swing to continue backward. There are a few other things to think of: the pivot is one; the right elbow another; but in my opinion the fewer things we can think of, the better we shall play.

I have a friend who has been trying to master the golf swing for fifteen years. Not long ago he told me it was a simple matter for him to concentrate on two or three things while attempting to hit the ball. I am certain that friend could play much better if he dismissed those thoughts and had but one on his mind, that one being *to hit the ball*, regardless of how he was going to hit it.

Reams have been written on the necessity of hitting the ball with the left hand. I have always contended, bearing in mind that most of us are right-handed players, that the real hitting is done with the right hand. In other words, let us suppose we have lost an arm. I feel certain that a golfer could get along far easier with his right arm than his left. The value of the left, in so far as I have been able to observe, is that of serving as guide, with the hitting power supplied entirely by the right forearm and hand. Arguments pro and con can be furnished along these lines, but after all what theory in golf will stand up without a discussion of some kind?

There are three recognized methods for gripping the club, and the choice among them should be made by the player himself. The oldest grip of all is the V. Next is the interlocking grip, which is taken by inserting the little finger of the right hand between the first two fingers of the left. Then there is the Vardon grip, which is by far the most popular of all. The Vardon grip is taken in the usual manner, with the exception that the little finger of the right hand is placed upon the knuckle of the forefinger of the left hand. Most of the star golfers employ the Vardon grip — such experts as Jones, Vardon himself, Hagen, and a host of others. I have for years pinned my faith to the interlocking grip. So has Gene Sarazen. But still other golfers of national and international prominence find the old-fashioned V grip good enough for them, outstanding players who use it being Abe Mitchell,

Sandy Herd, and Harrison Johnston. You can see by this that it is the man and not the grip, and the player himself is the one to make the final decision as to which of the three grips is best for him.

One thing I have noted in watching the younger players is this: they fail to make the proper differentiation between iron and wood club play. An iron club in their hands is handled in the same manner as a driver. There is a distinct difference in iron and wood club play. The wood should be played with a sweeping type of stroke. Distance can be got with a minimum expenditure of effort, all of which means a greater amount of accuracy. The iron shot, unless it has to be played with full power, should be more of a punch or hit than a sweep. To get the necessary crispness, a three-quarter stroke is more desirable. The three-quarter stroke makes the player hit, instead of making a sweep. The hit or punch insures accuracy, and, because the swing has been abbreviated, makes for a shot that will come closer to the line intended. Furthermore, the punch gives more compactness and therefore insurance that the ball will come to a stop quickly upon hitting the green or turf.

Such practices as imparting cut or draw to a ball are something that only the most expert should bother with. They have their value, but come only after hard practice and years of experience during which time the player has mastered control of club over ball.

I would place considerable importance on the recovery shot from the sand traps, because this is one of the real stroke-savers in the game. Most average golfers have a dreadful time playing out of a trap, and yet it is the coarsest shot in the game, one of the least skillful. The average player in a trap seems to think he must hit the ball in order to get it out and to the green. That is exactly what he should not do. His problem is that of hitting well behind the ball. A spot should be selected in back of the ball. Then the niblick-head should be driven at that spot. As the club-head reaches the sand, it passes underneath the ball and from there the ball is literally blown upward and out of the trap. There are times when a trap may not have sand enough below the ball to make it possible to play such a stroke, which is known as the explosion shot. The feeling of the sand underneath the feet will inform the player whether it is safe to blast the ball out. Since most traps near a green have plenty of sand, it is good policy to play the explosion shot to the exclusion of all others.

No man living can make a player keep his eye on the ball, and still this is the underlying secret of successful play. There are times when a golfer can hit a good shot without seeing the ball, but these times are few and far between. It is the very essence of good golf — keeping the eye on the ball. If every player could only make himself do this, he would hit mighty few poor shots. Lifting the eye off the ball often brings about a dozen faults, the most fatal of all being that of moving the body, a death-blow to the shot. And it is just as necessary to look at the ball on the tiniest putt as it is to concentrate upon doing so with the tee shot.

In summing up the salient things to concentrate upon while attempting to hit the ball accurately, I would make these suggestions: See that the ball is located in a position directly off the left heel. Then make up your mind to look at the ball. See it. Grip the club gently and assume a relaxed or sloppy condition, with the arms, legs, and body. This will tend to eliminate a certain measure of tenseness and provide a more satisfactory feeling at the moment of contact. And if you do not believe that tenseness is a poison in so far as hitting a ball is concerned, just go out some day and try to get yourself into the most tense position imaginable. Try to squeeze the grip as tight as you can and have your body as stiff as a poker, and watch the result.

AFTERWORD

OF ALL the words written about Francis Ouimet, none are more telling and enduring than Herbert Warren Wind's summary about his impact on the game. He said, "The luckiest thing, however, which happened to American golf, was that its first great hero was a person like Francis Ouimet."

Wind, considered America's greatest golf writer, wrote the Ouimet analysis in his classic, *The Story of American Golf,* in 1948. He described Ouimet, saying, "He was a fine man. He never allowed his successes to swell his head. He remained free from affectation. He was an instinctive gentleman. He was the great boy who became a great man. If the hero-worshipping American boy accidentally learned some of the 'real details' about his heroes in baseball and football, his ideals were frequently shattered. The more Americans learned about Francis Ouimet, the more they admired him."

Wind's words reveal much that may be missing from Ouimet's autobiography — Francis was so free from affectation and so sincerely humble that speaking or writing about himself was a difficult task. His book is not a "tell-all" or "brag sheet" for talk shows or tabloids. Yet his self-effacing nature should not hide the fact that Ouimet was one of the true giants of his game and American sports. He has been recognized with nearly every honor golf can bestow.

There is a great paradox in *A Game of Golf* that is a recurring theme in Ouimet's life. Although he achieved legendary status with his 1913 U.S. Open victory, it was his love of amateur golf and its crown, the United States Golf Association's Amateur Championship, that was his greatest joy and brass ring. While this book gives a solid description of his Open championship, it also recounts his exuberance at winning the 1914 U.S. Amateur championship, and concludes with his return to win the Amateur again seventeen years later. Ouimet wrote his autobiography the following year in 1932. This is an overview of the remaining thirty-five years of his life, his impact, how he was regarded, and how he is remembered.

Ouimet was a highly respected "career amateur," something that does not really exist in sports today. He had a business career and a family, and had to carefully "pick his spots" in determining his competitive schedule. Regardless, Ouimet became a household name with his Open title and emerged to join Jack Dempsey, Babe Ruth, and fellow golfer Bobby Jones as the early giants of sports. It was a golden age of sports, a period long before television and million-dollar purses, agents and mega-endorsements, card and autograph shows. Society was not as driven by professional athletes, their fortunes, and celebrity as it is today, and sports did not have the financial base it has now. In any event, the amateur golfer was held in higher regard than the professional golfer. During the years of this book, only Bobby Jones was a better amateur player, and Jones is considered the greatest amateur, and one of the greatest players, who ever lived.

Ouimet's competitive golf record is impeccable. In addition to his historic U.S. Open title, he won amateur championships in 1914 and 1931. During the years in between, a controversial rescinding of his amateur status, World War I, and the dominance of Jones thwarted his quest. Jones finally retired from competitive golf after his Grand Slam in 1930. From 1923 to 1932, Ouimet reached the semifinals of the U.S. Amateur an astounding seven times during a period when many of the best players did not turn pro. He played in the semifinals nine times and the finals three times. Three of Ouimet's semifinal losses were to Jones, who also had nine semifinal appearances and was the only golfer to have as many. Ouimet also captured the Crump Cup at Pine Valley and other top amateur invitational titles that came long before the USGA's Mid-Amateur existed but were competitively on a par with the Mid-Am. By today's standards Ouimet would probably have ranked in the top three amateurs for at least fifteen years — an unparalleled accomplishment.

Francis Ouimet was not a controversial man.

A GAME OF GOLF

Having his amateur status rescinded by the USGA in 1916 must have been painful to him. He makes scant mention of it in this book. The Western Golf Association in those days was comparable to the USGA in the Midwest and the Western Amateur and Open titles were considered what were later thought of as "majors." The WGA did not agree with the USGA's limited amateur eligibility requirements and invited Ouimet to the 1917 Western Amateur Championship, which he won. This fueled a public outcry against the USGA's rules. But World War I intervened and Ouimet joined the U.S. Army. He was assigned to special duty. He became one of the largest fund-raisers for the Red Cross through an extensive series of golf exhibitions. At the conclusion of the war, he was honored with the American Red Cross Prize Medal "in recognition of aid in humanity." The USGA rewrote its amateur rules, reinstating the popular American hero in 1918, but the competitive golfing banishment and the war came at the peak of his career.

The Walker Cup vs. Britain was a special domain for Ouimet. He either played on or was the non-playing captain of the first twelve Walker Cup matches, with an 11–1 team record in that period. Only Jay Sigel, with nine playing appearances (one more than Ouimet), played more. But the event did not begin until 1922, nine years after Ouimet's Open victory, which could make it a false compari-

278

son. After captaining the 1949 team, Ouimet retired. He received one of golf's ultimate honors two years later. He was the first American captain of the Royal and Ancient Golf Club of St. Andrews, which signified him as an international golfing good-will ambassador.

Ouimet was a hero in Boston. His 1913 U.S. Open victory has been selected as one of the top ten moments in Boston sports history. He could afford to play only a limited golf schedule, so he could not compete in as many Massachusetts Golf Association championships as he might have wished. Even so, he won six Massachusetts Amateur crowns (one behind Fred Wright's record), and was one of the few amateurs to win the Massachusetts Open in 1932.

"Senior Golf" did not emerge as a major competitive arena until long after Ouimet's prime, so he never had an opportunity to win at that level, yet he played well into his seventies. Oyster Harbors Club started a Danforth Memorial fourball tournament in 1965, two years before his death. Despite skepticism of its drawing power, it quickly sold out when word got around that Francis Ouimet would play. He became an honorary member of many clubs in the Boston area, and was frequently called on to play in exhibitions that opened new courses. He is wonderfully remembered as the main speaker at The Country Club's 1932 Fiftieth Anniversary Dinner, and he later played in TCC's esteemed matches against the Royal Montreal Club as a revered honorary member.

As great a player as Ouimet was, it was his genuine warmth, good humor, sportsmanship, and concern for others that made him so beloved. If golf is known for its gentlemanly behavior, much of the credit, at least in this country, belongs to him. He was complimentary of his opponents and playing partners almost to a fault. He would say "great shot" to a bladed iron that somehow rolled close to the pin, and there were times you might even wonder who won. The taunting and "in your face" attitude of some of today's athletes would horrify him. Ouimet affirmed his position as a gentleman and sportsman when he won the first Bob Jones Award for Distinguished Sportsmanship in 1955.

Ouimet's business career alternated between financial investment and "sports management." For a short time in the mid-teens, he co-owned a Boston sporting goods store with his brother-in-law, John Sullivan, which precipitated the USGA's rescinding of his amateur status. There were even "Francis Ouimet clubs" made that are now collectibles. In later years, he was president of the Boston Bruins, vice president of the Boston Braves baseball team (before it moved to Milwaukee and ultimately to Atlanta), and chairman of the Boston Arena Authority (now Northeastern University's

Matthews Arena) when it was a major Boston sporting site. He even dabbled in one of the first "television stores." For the most part, however, he was an
investment manager, usually working with his
friend the financial giant Bill Danforth. He finished
his career with Brown Brothers Harriman, where he
worked until his death in 1967. Today, the conference room is named after him. At Brown Brothers
he worked with Prescott Bush, who was USGA
president and the son-in-law of Herbert Walker, the
USGA president who contributed the Walker Cup.
Prescott Bush eventually became a U.S. Senator
from Connecticut and father of the forty-first and
grandfather of the forty-third Presidents of the
United States.

Ouimet was interested in helping young people.
He often spoke to young caddies, calling them
"Master Jones" or "Master Smith," and seemed gen-
uinely interested in their lives. His decision to stick
with ten-year-old Eddie Lowery as his caddie in the
1913 U.S. Open playoff is one of the great stories in
golf history. The romantic version has Francis
speaking with the members while Eddie stands a
few feet away. Upon seeing a single tear roll down
Eddie's crestfallen face, Francis announces that he'll
stick with the precocious boy. He and Lowery stayed
friends their entire lives, and Lowery went onto a
life of golfing and business success.

Ouimet also mentored young golfers. He took

Bobby Jones under his wing, and is said to have "straightened him out" after an emotional display at St. Andrews. He encouraged him through many of his major championship victories. He also worked with Gene Sarazen. "The Squire" spoke many times of how Ouimet counseled him to use his talent. He served as a pallbearer at Ouimet's funeral. As he paid his last respects he said, "Fast greens, Francis," something Ouimet would have appreciated.

Ouimet's achievements have been recognized in many ways. He was one of the first four inductees into the PGA Golf Hall of Fame in 1941 (with Walter Hagen, Bobby Jones, and Gene Sarazen). Today, a life-size statue of the Ouimet and Lowery image sculpted by Bob Pack stands at the entrance to the World Golf Hall of Fame in St. Augustine, Florida. He is one of three golfers (with Bobby Jones and Babe Didrickson Zaharias) to appear on a U.S. Postage Stamp.

The United States Golf Association recognizes Ouimet's 1913 victory as the most important moment in American golf history and it has honored him in numerous ways. It used the Ouimet and Lowery image as the logo for its centennial in 1995. It dedicated a room to Francis Ouimet in its museum in New Jersey, and has named its Senior Open trophy after him. The USGA held its 1963 U.S. Open at The Country Club in celebration of the fiftieth anniversary of the 1913 championship. Ouimet was the honorary chairman. He presented the winner's trophy to another native New Englander, Julius Boros, who defeated Jackie Cupit and Arnold Palmer. The 1988 Open was also held at TCC to celebrate the seventy-fifth anniversary. The postage stamp was released at that event. At the 1999 Ryder Cup at The Country Club, the USGA unveiled a life-size statue of Ouimet and Lowery near the first tee, where the photo from which it is patterned was shot. The statue was moved to its permanent location at Brookline's municipal course, Putterham Meadows, in 2000.

The other famous image of Ouimet is the "Red Jacket" portrait. By tradition when a new captain is inducted, the Royal and Ancient Golf Club of St. Andrews commissions a portrait of the captain wearing the "Red Jacket" attire and Queen Adelaide medal. It also holds a "driving in" ceremony. In both instances, Ouimet started traditions of his own, which reflected the reverence in which he was held.

The "driving in" ceremony is held on the first tee of St. Andrews. The new captain hits the opening drive of the fall meeting before an assembly of citizens of the old town. When the captain hits the ball a cannon is fired. The St. Andrews caddies wait along the fairway, trying to retrieve the ball and take it to the new captain. He then will "buy it back" with a gold Roman coin. When Ouimet was "driven in," he stood at the tee with legendary Royal and

Ancient pro Laurie Auchterlonie. He hit a Spalding ball specially stamped with an American eagle and a British lion, and presented a 1913 U.S. silver dollar, commemorative of his playoff with Vardon and Ray, in lieu of the gold coin. The gesture was wonderfully received.

There are several versions of Ouimet's "Red Jacket" portrait. The first was made in Scotland after Ouimet sat for photos in his home in Wellesley, Massachusetts. It hung for many years at the Royal and Ancient Golf Club.

Later, Eddie Lowery and Bill Danforth commissioned premier American portrait artist Thomas Stephens to paint a version for the Ouimet Room at the USGA Museum. Since Danforth and Lowery were both members of Augusta National, they sent "progress photos" of the portrait to Augusta National major domo Clifford Roberts. Roberts showed the photos to General Dwight Eisenhower, also an Augusta member. Roberts had been trying to convince the retired general that he, Eisenhower, could paint. Eisenhower, as a friend and great fan of Ouimet's, was especially interested in the photos. So it was arranged for Stephens to sit with Eisenhower for several days. He taught him the basics of painting and Eisenhower soon became quite adept. He eventually created his own version of the "Red Jacket" portrait and signed it, "Copy DE." Eisenhower gave the painting to Augusta

National as a statement of thanks for their role in helping him acquire his painting skills, and it hung for many years at the club. After Eisenhower died, the painting was given to the Royal and Ancient Club, and it replaced the original in their library. The original now hangs in the British Golfing Museum.

The great honor of Ouimet's becoming the first American captain (or president) of the Royal and Ancient, the world's largest golf governing body, is somewhat lost today. It came shortly after the end of World War II, following Ouimet's term on the USGA Executive Committee and as U.S. Walker Cup captain. It was an acknowledgment that he had done everything right as a competitor and team captain. The "Red Jacket" portrait recognized Ouimet as a gentleman and symbolized his international golfing goodwill efforts. It is in that spirit that the portrait has been reproduced so many times, and why Ouimet's name may have been better known in the British Isles than it was here in the United States.

The establishment in 1949 of the Francis Ouimet Scholarship Fund gave Ouimet more pleasure and pride than any honor he received. Founded by friends of Ouimet and the Massachusetts Golf Association, the scholarship was originally funded by a one-dollar increase per person of the annual MGA handicap fee. In the first year, there were thirteen scholarships awarded, for a total of $4,600. As this book goes to press, The Ouimet Fund awards nearly $1 million annually, and has given $15 million to more than 4,000 students in four-year renewable, need-based scholarships since it began. Scholarship applicants must work at least two years as caddies or helpers in pro-shop or course-superintendent operations at Massachusetts clubs. The Ouimet Fund is a nonprofit organization, and the second largest of approximately forty "caddie funds" in the country (behind the Midwest-wide Evans Fund operated by the Western Golf Association). Its graduates have taken distinguished positions of leadership in business and professional careers. Ouimet is said to have penned its original slogan — "From what golf has given you, let's give something back to golf."

Francis Ouimet was quite supportive of the fund. Students looked forward to meeting him at its annual banquet, where Ouimet would play the piano and lead sing-alongs (he enjoyed singing, and was a member of a couple of Boston barbershop quartets).

The Ouimet Fund has grown in many ways. For years it occupied a small building at the Leo Martin Golf Course in Weston. Today it resides in the William F. Connell Golf House at the Tournament Players' Club of Boston in Norton, Massachusetts. Visitors can view videos of Ouimet, trophies, photos, correspondence, a copy of the Dwight Eisenhower "Red Jacket" portrait, the grandfather clock presented by the Town of Brookline after Ouimet won the 1931 U.S. Amateur, and other items of interest.

The annual Ouimet banquet and awards presentation has become one of the largest such events in the country. Since Arnold Palmer's guest speaker appearance in 1997, when the "Francis Ouimet Award for Lifelong Contributions to Golf" was born, the average attendance has exceeded 1,200. Guests and awardees have included Gene Sarazen, Ben Crenshaw, Curtis Strange, Ken Venturi, and Eddie Lowery, former president George H. W. Bush, Chi Chi Rodriguez, and Nancy Lopez. Ouimet's two daughters, Barbara McLean and Jane Salvi, and Cynthia Wilcox, the daughter of Eddie Lowery, have also attended. In 2001 Wilcox eloquently accepted an honor for her late father. She asked the audience, "What if Francis hadn't stayed with Eddie?" and addressed the importance of that singular act of kindness. It was a dramatic and touching message and earned a tremendous response. The Lowery family has endowed the Ouimet Fund's top caddie scholarship, and people throughout Massachusetts have permanently endowed numerous Ouimet awards. And, just as the banquet is a great success, the Ouimet Golf Marathon is also the largest such event in the United States.

Ouimet was a champion of education, yet he never graduated from high school. He left Brookline

High School in 1910 to help his family. But at the unveiling of the Ouimet-Lowery statue before the 1999 Ryder Cup at The Country Club, Brookline town officials, impressed by what they heard about Ouimet, decided to change that. For several years, the Brookline High School Athletic Hall of Fame had been trying to induct Ouimet, but the bylaws required inductees to be graduates of the school. Within a few months, the school committee voted to award him an honorary degree. It was presented to Ouimet's daughters at the rededication of the statue when it was moved to Brookline's Putterham Municipal Course the following June. In a separate athletic ceremony a few weeks later, he was inducted into the school's hall of fame.

Francis did not have a formal education, but he was a highly intelligent and well-spoken man who conversed freely with some of the most educated and urbane people in Boston. He was an accomplished writer. In addition to this book, he penned *Golf Facts for Young People*, in 1921, and edited *Rules of Golf*, a booklet, in 1948. Ouimet authored a series of articles for Country Life magazine in 1928 on putting and "nerves" in golf. He also wrote occasional articles for newspapers about major tournaments in which he did not compete. And, like many of his generation, he was a fine and frequent letter writer. He wrote often to Bobby Jones, and his letters have formed the basis for historical research on the relationship and Jones's historic career.

Ouimet also participated in golfing instructional efforts in the early 1930s. He participated in a joint Carnegie Institute–Massachusetts Institute of Technology study of the flight of the golf ball and was one of the first stroboscopic photography subjects. Those photo sessions and the research papers they generated are considered valuable scientific data.

Francis DeSales Ouimet died September 10, 1967, a few days after he suffered a heart attack. It was a big story in Boston, sharing space with the Red Sox "Impossible Dream" pennant chase. He was at his home in Wellesley during the attack, and called his daughter Jane to say he was sick. On the way to the Newton-Wellesley Hospital, he awoke to find medical personnel and police tending to him. Somewhat embarrassed, he said, "Such a fuss, you'd think I was Tony Conigliaro," referring to the Red Sox outfielder who'd suffered major injuries when was hit by a pitch a few weeks before.

A year after Ouimet's death, the Par Club, now known as the Francis Ouimet Society, a Ouimet special contributors' membership group was formed, and the Francis Ouimet Memorial Tournament was founded. The Ouimet Memorial has become one of the premier amateur invitational tournaments in the East. The fifty-four-hole event is played at three different courses in three days, with the final round being at Ouimet's home course, Woodland Golf Club in Newton. Gene Sarazen played in a special exhibition match the first two years of the tournament and served as honorary chairman until his death in 1999. Arnold Palmer succeeded Sarazen and has served in that role since. The tournament boasts two of the most impressive trophies in golf. The trophy for the overall competition has three clubs that belonged to Ouimet, Vardon, and Ray mounted on a wooden block. Hanging from the clubs are silver golf balls inscribed with the names and years of each tournament winner. It was inspired by the President's Putter trophy awarded at the annual tournament of the Oxford and Cambridge Society at Rye, England. The senior division of the tournament, named the Lowery Division, has a small version of the Ouimet and Lowery statue as its trophy.

This book was originally published in 1932, and then republished by the Ouimet Fund in 1963, just before the fiftieth anniversary of the Ouimet 1913 U.S. Open victory. For years, copies of the book were given to Ouimet scholars as graduation gifts. It was also given to all the participants in the 1968 USGA Junior Championship at The Country Club.

One of the recipients was a young Ben Crenshaw from Austin, Texas. Crenshaw was presented with the Francis Ouimet Award for Lifelong Contributions to Golf at the Ouimet Fund's Fiftieth Anniversary Banquet in 1999. He was also the

A Game of Golf

Ryder Cup captain that year, when the U.S. team beat the Europeans at The Country Club.

The night before the final round of the Ryder Cup, Crenshaw spoke to his team about the history of TCC, and about Francis Ouimet. When Justin Leonard sunk the winning putt on the seventeenth green, Crenshaw kissed the green where again history was made.

One of the millions of viewers at that moment was Mark Frost, who was immediately intrigued by the historical reference. Frost was a great storyteller, with his award-winning books and television shows such as *Hill Street Blues* and *Twin Peaks*. He recognized an untold story in that moment, and over the next few months worked with the USGA, the Ouimet Fund, The Country Club, and many other sources in developing his superb book, *The Greatest Game Ever Played*. The book has been hailed as one of the best golf books written, has gone through several printings, and has been awarded the USGA's International Book Award. In late 2003, Disney Pictures announced its plans for a full-length motion picture based on the book.

Before Francis Ouimet's Cinderella victory, golf was restricted to the wealthy and dominated by the English and Scots. He came from a poor family, but lived across the street from The Country Club — the pinnacle of Boston gentry. He started in golf as a caddie. Ouimet's youth, his being the first amateur to win the U.S. Open, his demeanor, and his unknown status formed as compelling a tale as any in sports history. Crowds never before seen on a golf course (with estimates as high as 15,000), came out to the playoff to root for the American boy turned local hero. With his victory, the Ouimet story spread like wildfire. Boston's seven daily newspapers were filled for days with words about this new hero, as were papers around the country and the world. His victory caused a great boom in golf and inspired millions to try the game.

Within a decade of his victory the number of American participants grew from 350,000 to more than 2,000,000. The number of courses tripled, and with municipal courses being built, people of all economic levels began playing. James Michael Curley, elected mayor of Boston in 1913, took up golf and played in several exhibitions with Ouimet. Curley was one of the great political figures of the twentieth century. He had the George Wright Golf Course built in the Hyde Park section of Boston. Donald Ross, a prolific and prominent architect, designed the municipal treasure. George Wright, a great Boston athlete and sportsman, had given Ouimet a job and the time off to play in 1913. The aptly named course must have given Ouimet great joy.

Ouimet was the first in a line of American golf heroes running from Bobby Jones, Gene Sarazen,

A Game of Golf

Sam Snead, and Ben Hogan, to Arnold Palmer, Jack Nicklaus, Lee Trevino, Tom Watson, and Tiger Woods. His match against Vardon and Ray was the first real international showdown, and it soon begat a Walker Cup and a Ryder Cup. Today Tiger Woods is considered a golfing "pied piper," having brought many new players into the game. But nearly a century earlier, Francis Ouimet overcame the American social taboos to bring the game to all people. He set the gentlemanly standard by which the game of golf is played (and possibly one of the reasons it is so scandal-free), and inspired the development of a scholarship fund that has helped thousands of young "Eddie Lowerys," as he did.

Francis Ouimet had a humble view of what he accomplished. This book gives insight into a kinder, gentler time when competition was more about friendship and camaraderie. Ouimet never bragged about himself. He never thought anything he did was a big deal. He left the world a much better place than the way he found it, and, in the end, that is all that any man can ever hope to do.

Ouimet's legacy is central to the game of golf as it stands today, yet most golfers probably don't know who Francis DeSales Ouimet was. Serious golf historians and officials around the world and the Ouimet Scholarship recipients however, know his name well. We are deeply indebted to the Northeastern University Press for helping us take another look at his world. Most of all, we are indebted to Francis Ouimet for being who he was.

ROBERT DONOVAN
EXECUTIVE DIRECTOR, FRANCIS OUIMET
SCHOLARSHIP FUND, INC.
JANUARY 2004